Youth
MINISTRY
IN CRISIS

BARRY R. HARKER, PH.D.

©Copyright 2004
by Barry R. Harker

All Rights Reserved
Printed in the USA

Published by
Hartland Publications
P. O. Box 1
Rapidan. VA 22733
www.hartlandpublications.com

Cover Design and Layout
by Kel Naughton

ISBN 0-923309-92-6

Dedication

*In memory
of
Pastor H. C. K. Harker (1877-1962)
beloved grandfather and man of God*

Table of Contents

Preface	i
Introduction	iv
Chapter 1: GODS AND GAMES	
Coming in from the Cold	1
Mimetic Magic	3
Sports of the Sky Wanderers	7
Sacred Sports	10
The Dualist Origins of Sports	14
Dissonance	19
Chapter 2: COSMIC THEATER	
Athletes of the Emotions	24
Drama	34
Dance	36
Tragicomedy	39
Masks, Mimes, Marionettes and Magicians	43
The Mirror of the Cosmos	46
Chapter 3: MARKING THE MUSIC	
The Rejection of Reason	51
The Return of Myth	65
Chapter 4: DIVIDED HEARTS	
Lovers of Pleasures	73
Cinema	75
Extreme Sports	78
Body Piercing and Decoration	81
Dress	84
Emotions	87
Addictions	92

Chapter 5: WANDERING STARS
    Farewell to Reason   96
    Dominion Theology   99
    Chronological Snobbery   101
    A Matter of Taste   103
    From the Heart   106
    There's Good in Every Voice   108
    Relevance   111
Chapter 6: FACING THE CRISIS
    Group Think   115
    Biblical Principles of Youth Ministry   117
    A Place To Stand   124
    Reformation   128
Epilogue   130
Bibliography   132
General Index   135
Scriptural Index   143
Hartland Publications   146

Preface

THIS BOOK EXAMINES the revolutionary ideas and practices that are transforming Christian youth ministry and reveals why these changes have brought youth ministry to a state of profound crisis. The changes are so pervasive and the betrayal of youth so complete that no attempt has been made to address specific circumstances or cases. Instead, the book focuses on testing these changes against Biblical principles. While the book highlights the contemporary debasement of youth ministry, it concludes by outlining the steps that must be taken if the crisis is to be resolved and youth ministry restored to a culture of defensible innovation.

The central point of *Youth Ministry in Crisis* is that the principle of cultural relevance, which is helpful within certain clearly defined limits in evangelism, is highly destructive when it is used to justify practices that are indefensible on Biblical grounds. Hence, the book is not arguing against the attempt to identify as closely as possible with those whom we seek to influence for the gospel. It does argue, however, that all innovation in youth ministry, like all innovation generally, must be brought to the test of the Bible. If the Bible has any authority in matters of belief and practice, it has authority in every matter touching our duty to God and man and its principles must be upheld and obeyed. It is unsafe to do otherwise, regardless of how attractive an alternative idea or practice may seem.

Much of the book is devoted to sports, theatre, rock music and other manifestations of popular culture in youth ministry. Many of the prevailing elements of youth ministry have ancient pagan roots and, as the meaning of something today is bound up with its origins, it is necessary to know something of the origins and history of these practices when evaluating them against Biblical principles. It is also important to understand how the early Christians related to these practices. With this type of historical information at our disposal, we are better equipped to differentiate the acceptable from the unacceptable. That is why an attempt has been made to situate the various ideas and practices under consideration in the larger historical context.

The introductory essay outlines the central themes and issues that are explored in this book and should be read first. It is desirable to read the chapters in sequence as the latter chapters build on the earlier ones. Chapter One situates the origins of sports in the dualistic religions that arose after the fall of mankind and identifies the links between ancient and modern sports. It reveals the fundamental incompatibility between the principles of sports and Christianity. Chapter Two examines the origin, purposes and meaning of theater and notes how theater, which began in ancient Greece, mirrors the Greek conception of the cosmos. It reveals significant similarities in the religious origins of theater and sports and shows why the use of theatrical devices in youth ministry today is indefensible.

Chapter Three exposes the significance of rock music and its variants in Christian youth ministry today, both from an historical and a prophetic perspective. Chapter Four outlines the dangers of adopting or legitimizing in youth ministry many of the central aspects of contemporary youth culture. Chapter Five evaluates the arguments that are used to support the revolutionary changes to youth ministry while Chapter Six examines Biblical principles of youth ministry and establishes some criteria for creating a defensible program of youth ministry.

The issues raised in this book are of central importance to the well being of the church. Already, the changes to youth ministry are impacting upon the church at large and the results are not encouraging. Everywhere there are signs that the church is facing a major identity crisis. Unless there is a change in direction, youth ministry is destined to bring the church into some hard places and to create a crisis in confidence in church leadership. The damage

Preface

caused to the fabric of the church will not be easily repaired. It is time to subject the ideas and practices that are driving youth ministry to a searching examination in the light of God's word.

Biblical references are included in the text and, unless otherwise noted, all Biblical quotations are from the King James Version. Authorities are generally cited in accordance with the Chicago Manual of Style Citation Guide. Electronic sources are acknowledged in the endnotes of relevant chapters. I am grateful to my wife, Cecily, for her encouragement and assistance during the preparation of this book, to my friend, Kel Naughton, for the cover design, and to Mrs. Faith Lyons, the Director of Hartland Publications, for guiding the project to its completion.

YOUTH MINISTRY IN CRISIS

Introduction

THE OLD TESTAMENT TESTIFIES that the chosen people of God were directed to separate themselves from the religious practices and traditions of the surrounding nations and to obey the commandments of God. Through separation and obedience, God intended that His people demonstrate the benefits of obedience to Him. As the nations were drawn to the wisdom and understanding of the Israelites, the knowledge of God and salvation was to be disseminated throughout the world.

When the Jewish nation demonstrated its persistent rejection of Jesus Christ by stoning Stephen, God rejected the Jews as his chosen people. The duty to spread the knowledge of God throughout the world passed to the Christian believers: "But ye are a chosen generation, a royal priesthood, an holy nation, a peculiar people; that ye should shew forth the praises of him who hath called you out of darkness into his marvellous light: Which in time past were not a people, but are now the people of God: which had not obtained mercy, but now have obtained mercy" (1 Peter 2:9, 10).

On the eve of His crucifixion, in His great intercessory prayer, Jesus endorsed the theme of separation from the world and obedience to all the revealed will of God: "I pray not that thou shouldest take them out of the world, but thou shouldest keep them from the evil. They are not of the world, even as I am not of the world. Sanctify them through thy truth: thy word is truth" (John 17:15-17). Clearly, it is God's plan that Christians in all eras bring their lives into conformity with the truth as revealed in the Bible. All beliefs and practices must be brought to the test of God's word.

A failure to do so will bring spiritual weakness and endanger the church's mission in the world.

That is why the issue of separation and obedience is a constant concern of the New Testament writers. John writes: "Love not the world, neither the things that are in the world. If any man love the world, the love of the Father is not in him. For all that is in the world, the lust of the flesh, and the lust of the eyes, and the pride of life, is not of the Father, but is of the world. And the world passeth away, and the lust thereof: but he that doeth the will of God abideth for ever" (1 John 2:15-17). John goes on to reveal that separation and obedience are the result of true faith in Jesus Christ (1 John 5:1-5).

For the early Christians, separation and obedience meant resisting many of the beliefs and practices that made the classical civilizations of Greece and Rome among the most alluring and influential in history. Greek language and philosophy saturated the Mediterranean. Greco-Roman art and architecture had enormous visual appeal. Sports, theater and music were extremely popular. Many of the most appealing aspects of these cultures derived from the practices of pagan religions. The visual appeal of these cultural manifestations of pagan religions greatly encouraged "the lust of the flesh, the lust of the eyes, and the pride of life."

In this context, it is perhaps understandable that some of the Christian converts had difficulty in putting away the beliefs and practices that had characterized their former lives. The apostle Paul had occasion to warn the Colossians: "Beware lest any man spoil you through philosophy and vain deceit, after the tradition of men, after the rudiments of the world, and not after Christ" (Colossians 2:8). Philosophy attempts to explain reality and the nature of things through human reasoning alone. Paul warns the Colossians to avoid all forms of thought that begin with the primacy of human reason or human tradition.

Paul also faced the problem of idolatry in the fledgling church.

Introduction

Once, he used the experience of the Israelite idolatry in the wilderness as a warning to the Corinthian believers and to Christians until the end of time (1 Corinthians 10:1-11). He pointed out the debasing effects of improper leisure activities: "Neither be ye idolaters, as were some of them; as it is written, The people sat down to drink, and rose up to play. Neither let us commit fornication, as some of them committed, and fell in one day three and twenty thousand" (Verses 7, 8). The careless revelry of the Israelites led to the worship of the golden calf. Paul warns the Corinthians to avoid activities that lead to idolatry. He completes his warning with this appeal: "Wherefore, my dearly beloved, flee from idolatry" (Verse 14).

In Corinth, one of the popular pastimes associated with idolatry was Greek athletics. Isthmia, the site of one of the four major athletic festivals of ancient Greece, was just a few miles from Corinth. Like all athletic festivals in ancient Greece, the Isthmian Games were intimately associated with religion. In fact, the worship of Zeus at the ancient Olympic Games was the highest expression of ancient Greek religion. So popular were the Isthmian games that Paul based one of his most memorable metaphors on the events that took place there (1 Corinthians 9:24-27).

The athletes who competed at Isthmia engaged in strenuous training, ate special diets and took adequate rest and sleep. Many used special performance-enhancing herbs to give them a competitive edge. They did this in order to obtain the crown of wild celery that was given to winners at Isthmia. Paul used the extreme effort expended in pursuit of this corruptible crown to emphasize the spiritual effort needed to secure the incorruptible crown of eternal life. Some have interpreted Paul's athletic metaphor as approval of Greek athletics but this position is not tenable in the light of the intimate association between sports and religion in ancient Greece.

There is another compelling reason why Paul's use of athletic

Youth Ministry In Crisis

metaphors should not be interpreted as approval of Greek athletics. The gymnasia where Greek men gathered to exercise naked and to socialize were associated with pederasty and homosexuality. Paul clearly rejected these sinful practices: "Know ye not that the unrighteous shall not inherit the kingdom of God? Be not deceived: neither fornicators, nor idolaters, nor adulterers, nor effeminate, nor abusers of themselves with mankind, nor thieves, nor covetous, nor drunkards or revilers, nor extortioners, shall inherit the kingdom of God. And such were some of you: but ye are washed, but ye are sanctified, but ye are justified in the name of the Lord Jesus, and by the Spirit of our God" (1 Corinthians 6:9-11).

In addition to Greek athletics, there are at least two other categories of leisure practices in Corinth that are encompassed in Paul's warning in 1 Corinthians 10:1-11. Like Greek athletics, both categories of activities were immensely appealing and popular. Both categories were associated with Greek religion and thus with idolatry. The first category is theater. Greek drama originated in the yearly rites in honour of the resurrection of Dionysus or Bacchus, the Greek god of wine. The second category is the music associated with the frenzy, sexual license and ecstatic behavior of Dionysian festivals. These categories of activities, by their intimate association with pagan religion, were to be avoided, for everything that a Christian does is to be done to the glory of God.

At the spring festival held in honour of Dionysus in Athens, known as the Greater Dionysia, three poets, selected in competition, presented a tragedy and a satyr[1] play — "a farcical, often bawdy parody of the gods and their myths."[2] Comedy, which developed in the fifth century B. C., was added later. The oldest comedies have a highly formal structure thought to be derived from ancient fertility rites. The humor was associated with bawdy, satirical attacks on public figures, scatological jokes, and parodies of the gods.

Christians in the first century A. D. largely heeded the warn-

Introduction

ings against compromise with Greco-Roman philosophy, religion and culture. The early Christians shunned the athletic festivals, theaters, music and entertainments of the Roman world. Sadly, things changed. From the second to the fifth centuries, Platonic ideas were adopted by influential church fathers, Justin Martyr, Clement, Origen and Augustine, leading to the corruption of Biblical Christianity, especially at Alexandria and Rome. Roman Christianity led the way in adapting pagan rituals and festivals to its use in order to enhance its influence. No doubt much of the early compromise with paganism was done in sincerity but the results were disastrous for Christianity and the unity of the faith.

The failure to uphold the Biblical principles of separation and obedience allowed the world to march into the church. Centuries of tyranny, conflict, confusion and weakness flowed from this failure. The course of Western civilization was dramatically changed. Instead of a uniquely Judeo-Christian culture in the West, the compromise with pagan religion, philosophy and culture set up a tension in the West between Judeo-Christianity and the heritage of the classical civilizations of Greece and Rome. The contradictions in Western civilization are traceable to this accommodation between Christianity and paganism. How different the course of Western history might have been if Christianity had remained consistently true to its Biblical basis.

The classical civilizations of Greece and Rome are polar opposites of Biblical Christianity. Greece and Rome stand for human achievement, ceaseless competition, the delight of the senses and self-sufficient individualism. On the other hand, Biblical Christianity enjoins dependence upon God, overriding concern for the interests of all, sublimation of passion to morality and the values of the spiritual life. Classical civilization represents the holiness of beauty and Biblical Christianity represents the beauty of holiness. That is why Matthew Arnold, the nineteenth century English poet, could say that Hellenism[3] and Hebraism are the two points between which "the human spirit must forever oscillate" (Jenkyns 1980, 68).

The vitality of Christianity has always been dependent upon its separation from the manifestations of pagan culture and its obedience to God's revealed word. After centuries of disastrous compromise with paganism, the Protestant Reformation began to restore many of the Biblical beliefs and practices that had been rejected or encrusted with centuries of tradition. Progressively, Protestantism looked more and more like the simple Biblical Christianity of the Waldenses that had survived centuries of persecution. The word of God was central to the worship and evangelism of the Waldenses during the Dark and Middle Ages. Even today, visitors to the Waldensian valleys of the Cottian Alps in northern Italy will find a simple church architecture based upon the central place of the preaching of God's word in worship.

Significantly, the Reformation had a major impact upon sports, theater and music. Wherever Protestantism took effect, there were "strenuous attempts to curtail public amusements, sports, the arts, or the pleasurable use of leisure" (Kraus, 1971, 152). Protestantism also had a dramatic effect on medieval miracle plays, which combined Biblical scenes and comedy. Religious drama in northern Europe was in severe decline by the middle of the sixteenth century. Protestantism also made a considerable impact on music. Congregational singing was introduced and hymns were sung to express Biblical faith. The Bible was made accessible to the people and Protestantism brought a revival of piety and prosperity. The cultural legacy of the Reformation is seen in the work of such towering figures as Rembrandt Van Rijn, John Milton, Johann Sebastian Bach and John Bunyan.

Today, the flame of the Reformation is all but extinguished. In an age of Darwinism, higher criticism, materialism and hedonism, many contemporary Christians find the Biblical concepts of separation from the world and obedience to all the revealed will of

Introduction

God irrelevant or quaint. In the main, Protestant identity has been overtaken by a bland ecumenism that shuns doctrinal distinctiveness. Weakened by a loss of identity and often membership, and weary from the prolonged battle with popular culture, many Protestant churches have decided to make the best of a bad thing and have adopted the norms and practices of the world in the name of cultural relevance. Rock music, magic, drama, comedy, clowning, mime, puppetry, sports, Olympism, extreme adventure activities, movies, dancing and youth fashions in the churches have made much of Christianity indistinguishable from popular culture. The effects can be seen most readily in the radical transformation of youth ministry and evangelism.

A little reflection will reveal that the practices that are being embraced with such fervor in much of contemporary Christianity fall broadly into the three categories of activities that were shunned by the early Christians—sports, theater and Dionysian music. Compromise with these religious and cultural manifestations of the classical world helped bring early Christianity to the point of crisis and contributed to the need for the Protestant Reformation. Therefore, it would be historically naïve to think that the wholehearted embrace of sports, theater, rock music and pop culture by Christianity today can take place without engendering a crisis of similar magnitude.

There are few indications, if any, that those churches that have embraced cultural relevance in youth ministry and evangelism recognize its long-term dangers. It is generally understood that youth constitute the future of a church. That is why churches now place so much emphasis on retaining their youth. The adoption of cultural relevance as a guiding principle in youth ministry is designed to stem the loss of youth from the churches. Yet, it is clear that insufficient attention has been given to the implications of retaining youth in the church whose tastes have been radically altered by accommodation to worldly values.

Youth Ministry In Crisis

The serious difficulty with the principle of cultural relevance in youth ministry is that, having once accepted the principle that it is necessary to be like the world to influence the world, a clear rejection of Biblical principles, there are no benchmarks to determine at what point the adoption of popular culture by church youth is fatally prejudicial to the larger church culture. Under these circumstances, profound and, in many cases, irreversible changes can occur to a church before most have the least hint that there is a problem.

An unintended consequence is no less harmful because it is unintended. Church history reveals that compromise with popular culture never brings the world closer to the church but always brings the church closer to the world. The world in the church is never harmless. Whenever the church permits the world to invade its precincts or whenever it embraces the world as a policy, weakness and confusion result. The adoption of cultural relevance as a guiding principle in youth ministry and evangelism is an invitation to failure. The likely extent of that failure can be seen in terms of the threat that cultural relevance poses to God's stated purposes.

Before His ascension, Jesus gave His disciples the commission: "Go ye therefore, and teach all nations, baptizing them in the name of the Father, and of the Son, and of the Holy Ghost: Teaching them to observe all things whatsoever I have commanded you: and, lo, I am with you alway, even unto the end of the world. Amen" (Matthew 28:19, 20). Earlier, Jesus revealed that He would not come again, nor the world end, until the gospel had been preached in the entire world as a witness to all nations (Matthew 24:14). The gospel that is to go to the entire world and that is to be taught to all nations includes the observance of all things that Jesus has commanded. The peoples of the world are to be taught that the gospel requires them to separate from the evil practices of the world and to be obedient to God (John 17:15-17; 1 John 2:15-17). Thus, when a church adopts the principle of cultural

Introduction

relevance and embraces worldly practices, and fails to obey God, it undermines its capacity to fulfill the gospel commission.

A church that embraces cultural relevance also encourages its members in a fatal delusion. When Jesus comes the second time, there will be many professing Christians who will be denied entrance to heaven because they failed to obey God: "Not everyone who saith unto me, Lord, Lord, shall enter the kingdom of heaven; but he that doeth the will of my father which is in heaven. Many will say to me in that day, Lord, Lord, have we not prophesied in thy name? and in thy name have cast out devils? and in thy name done many wonderful works? And then will I profess unto them, I never knew you: depart from me ye who work iniquity" (Matthew 7:21-23). Iniquity is sin and sin is the transgression of the law (Isaiah 59:2; 1 John 3:4). Those who are denied entrance to heaven are those who do not consider it essential to obey God's law or His requirements. Yet, as Jesus pointed out, it is futile to claim a saving relationship with Him while disobeying any of His commandments or precepts. If we call Jesus, Lord, we must do what He says (Luke 6:46).

While obedience does not cause salvation, it is an indispensable condition of salvation (Romans 8:1-14). When sin entered the world, God's image in humanity was defaced. Obedience is part of God's plan to restore His image in humanity. That it is God's plan to restore His moral image in humanity is confirmed by Jesus: "Be ye therefore perfect, even as your Father which is in heaven is perfect" (Matthew 5:48). The restitution of all things begins when Jesus comes again (Acts 3:20, 21). Yet, before that takes place, we must repent and have our sins blotted out (Acts 3:19). The blotting out of our sins is part of the vindication of God's character and is accomplished before Jesus comes through sanctified obedience (Isaiah 43:25; Revelation 22:11-15). The blotting out of sins completes the restoration of God's moral image in His people (Romans 8:29). The principle of cultural relevance works

Youth Ministry In Crisis

in direct opposition to this desirable outcome.

Thus, the principle of cultural relevance in youth ministry is destructive in several critical dimensions relevant to the spiritual health of a church and its members. By obstructing the transmission of truth to the younger generation in a church, cultural relevance causes confusion, weakness and loss of mission. It also fosters the delusion that it is a light thing to keep God's commandments, thereby hindering the preparation that individuals need to make to meet Jesus in peace when He comes. Additionally, it works against God's plan to restore His moral image in His people. Therefore, those who embrace cultural relevance unfit themselves to receive the finishing touch of immortality when Jesus comes (1 Corinthians 15:51-56).

In this context, so close to the Lord's second coming, it is hard to imagine a more effective way to frustrate God's purposes than to embrace the notion that a church must become like the world to retain its youth and fulfill its evangelistic responsibilities. Yet, cultural relevance is being embraced with a vengeance and the results are often bizarre. It is a difficult climate in which to question contemporary trends in youth ministry, but our young people are too important to be abandoned to ideas and practices that are destructive of Biblical faith.

Notes
[1] A satyr is one of a class of Greek woodland deities in human form with horse's ears and a tail.
[2] Encarta 1993, Drama and Dramatic Arts.
[3] Hellenism is imitation of the Greeks.

Chapter 1

GODS AND GAMES

Coming in from the Cold

Few ideals have achieved such widespread acceptance in modern Christianity and yet are more at odds with the spirit of Christ than competitive sports. The spirit of supremacy, of which competitive sports are a visible manifestation, is incompatible with the principles of the kingdom of heaven. Yet, competitive sports are widely regarded in the Christian world as desirable activities. It is lamentable that the spirit of self exaltation should be so evident among the professed people of God today.

Despite the almost reverential way in which many Christians treat sports today, it is important to note that competitive sports are a relative newcomer to Christian legitimacy. After centuries of prohibition, disapproval or grudging toleration by Christian leaders, sports finally achieved Christian respectability in mid-nineteenth England, courtesy of the emerging Muscular Christianity movement (Harker, 1996). As the Muscular Christian ideals of friendly competition, fair play, and sportsmanship were exported to the world, the groundwork for amateur sport and the revival of the ancient Olympic Games was laid. Significantly, it is to the time when the values of Muscular Christianity began to prevail in the churches that we can also trace the modern origins of the current crisis in youth ministry.

Sports may have come late to Christian legitimacy but, when they were brought in from the cold, they were embraced with a vengeance. In many places, especially in the British public schools,[1] sports were quickly appropriated for the purpose of Christian character development. Previously, character development among the young was seen to result from reading the Bible and moral literature and attending chapel or church. The changing emphasis in character development may have seemed innocent at first but it marked the beginning of a period of compromise that resulted in an unprecedented debasement of Biblical principles of youth ministry in the early twenty-first century.

The rapidity with which competitive sports took over the domains of moral education, youth ministry and public morality is noticeable in developments between 1844 and 1888. In 1844, the Young Men's Christian Association (YMCA) was formed in England, reaching the United States of America in 1851. By the 1880s the YMCA had established some 260 large gymnasiums in the cities of the United States, becoming a leader in sport as a mass movement. A similar change occurred between 1844 and 1859 in American universities and colleges. The Manual Labor movement[2] in American higher education went into a sharp decline in 1844, resulting within 15 years in the appearance of gymnasiums in most universities and colleges. By the end of the mid-Victorian era in Britain, the belief that games produced Christian gentlemen had taken root in society at large. When, in 1888, Baron Pierre de Coubertin conceived the idea of reviving the ancient Olympic Games, he had strong support in the English-speaking world for the ideals that he wished to incorporate in the revived Olympic Games.

The inclusion of a muscular morality in Christianity did more than add another dimension to Christian character development. It radically altered the Christian landscape. Sport provided an early impetus to ecumenism by providing Roman Catholics and Protestants with a common passion. The lack of Biblical warrant for athletic competition helped to undermine the Biblical basis of Protestantism. By opening the door to the principles of ancient Greek athletics, Protestantism set itself to repeat the compromises with paganism that beset Roman Christianity in the early centuries of the Christian era. To understand how sports are debasing youth ministry today, it is important to understand the origins of sports.

Mimetic Magic

The best documented evidence of the association of competitive sports and religion is found in the ancient Olympic Games (McIntosh 1963, 3-4). The ancient Olympic Games were the highest expression of Greek religion. They were held at Olympia in honor of the god Zeus, the supreme god of ancient Greek mythology, and included sacrifices and religious rituals. Olympia takes its name from Mount Olympus in northern Greece. Mount Olympus was the home of the gods who were ruled over by Zeus. The Altis at Olympia, a grove of trees at the foot of Mount Kronos, was the most sacred place for the worship of Zeus in Greece. Within the Altis, before the worship of Zeus had become established, fertility rites to the earth Goddess, Ge, were practiced (Swaddling 1992, 7).

The first building in the Altis was the temple of Hera, dedicated to the fertility goddess who was known variably as the consort or sister of Zeus. Hera was also known as the queen of heaven, a title that identified her with the mother-goddess who was known by a variety of names in ancient cultures. It was worship of the queen of heaven that was one of the factors leading to the Babylonian captivity of the Jews of Judah (Jeremiah 7:18). Today, the Olympic flame is lit near the ruins of the temple of Hera. A woman, dressed as the chief priestess of Hera and accompanied by other women dressed as priestesses, has the honor of lighting the flame from the rays of the midday sun, using a concave mirror of burnished steel.

While the precise origins of the ancient Olympic Games are unknown, their close association with mimetic magic is strongly suggestive of a mimetic origin. Mimesis is imitation and mimetic magic is the attempt to control the forces of nature through imitation. A belief in mimetic magic ascribed to winners in athletic contests the power to bring fertility and growth to crops and stock (McIntosh 1963, 2). In primitive societies, the dead are often associated with powers of growth. Just as the blood shed by means of sacrifice is thought to refresh the dead for their labors, so the effort expended in sport was thought to be transferred to the powers of growth and fertility.

The theory that the ancient Olympic Games originated in mimetic magic has great explanatory value in terms of the legends about the Olympic Games and associated practices. Funeral games were common in early Greek culture. In the *Iliad*, Homer describes the funeral games for Patroklos in great detail. One of the legends connected with the Olympic Games suggests that they were originally funeral games in honor of Pelops. The association of games and death is illustrative of the identification of the powers of growth with death in mimetic magic. Pottery depicting sports is frequently found in ancient Greek graves. While the discovery of sporting iconography in graves may simply reflect the deceased's activities or aesthetic taste, or represent an idealized and successful life, it is consistent with the notion of funerary gifts or votive offerings to the gods (Measham, Donnelly and Spathari 2000, 25).

The discovery of a bull rhyton[3] from the early to middle Minoan period in Crete is evidence of an early association of funerary gifts and fertility (Measham, Donnelly and Spathari 2000, 25, 34). The bull rhyton contains human figures on the horns performing a bull-leaping routine and a human figure between the horns symbolizing human fertility. The heads of bulls have also been found juxtaposed with corpses in burial chambers, suggesting the theme of regeneration (Husain 1997, 14). The shape of the bull's head and its horns have been compared with the human uterus and fallopian tubes, so placing a body near a bull's head would be a way of preparing for its rebirth. Thus, the bull is associated with the themes of fertility and regeneration.

Bull leaping, which was known in Greece, was a contest involving bulls in which both young men and women took part, probably to a musical accompaniment. It has been suggested that bull leaping took place during fertility rituals or in honor of the gods Poseidon and Zeus. Either explanation is consistent with the later development of the ancient Olympic Games from fertility magic for, as we have seen, bulls were symbols of fertility and the games in honor of Zeus at Olympia were associated with fertility magic. The Priestess of Demeter Chamyne, a fertility goddess, was required to watch the games at Olympia seated on an altar placed on the northern side of the running track in the stadium. Thus, the early association of funerary gifts with athletic and fertility motifs in the bull rhyton from Crete supports the theory that locates the origin of athletic contests at Olympia in mimetic magic.

The sacrifice of the hundred oxen on the huge altar in front of the temple of Zeus at Olympia on the third day of the Olympic festival is almost certainly associated with fertility magic. The act of worshipping or placating Zeus, who is considered able to influence the forces of nature, by the ritual sacrifice of oxen, is consistent with mimetic magic. It is also consistent with the long association of Olympia with fertility rites. The enduring sacred nature of the contests that took place at Olympia, mirroring the ongoing Greek cultural obsession with competition, almost certainly invests the animal sacrifices to Zeus with continuing religious significance.

Moreover, the origin of the ancient Olympic Games in mimetic magic is able to explain the vegetation prizes at Olympia and at many other ancient Greek athletic festivals. While vigorous training was obviously important, it was thought that victory was only possible through the favor of the gods (Measham, Donnelly and Spathari 2000, 24). Winning was a sign of favor with the gods and indicated possible influence with them. That may help to explain why triple winners at Olympia were worshipped as gods. The association of winning and vegetation prizes at Olympia therefore points strongly to mimetic magic as the origin of the contests there. As we shall note shortly, the association of games and contests with fertility and regeneration of vegetation is documented in other ancient cultures.

One of the events at Olympia that hints at an origin in mimetic magic is the discus throw. Unlike most other events at Olympia, the discus throw does not have any particular military application or value. A relief of a discus thrower in the National Archaeological Museum of Athens shows a young discus thrower with a discus in his left hand. The head is projected against the circle of the discus. The discus is evocative of the sun. The association of the discus with the sun is not unlikely, given the association of the Olympic Games with fertility. The sun, often associated with the bull, is an important fertility symbol.

Yet, the strongest evidence that the ancient Olympic Games originated in mimetic magic is the time at which they were held. They always took place at the second or third full moon after the summer solstice (McIntosh 1963, 2). The date always fell between 6 August and 19 September by our reckoning because they were held every fiftieth and forty-ninth month to accommodate the ninety-nine lunar months that coincide approximately with eight solar years. The timing of the Olympic Games supports the theory that early races may have played a role in determining fertility and kingship.

The theory that the ancient Olympic Games originated in mimetic magic is not only supported by the intimate association between religion and athleticism in ancient Greece but also by the relationship between religion and sports in many early cultures. While the cultural manifestations of that relationship vary, there are significant similarities in the way early cultures attach religious importance to their sports and games. Even the trend to secularization over time, that is often evident in these early cultures, is not able to obliterate the cosmic dimensions of these games. Compelling examples of the cultic origins of sports can be found in the ball games of early Central America. It is to these ball games that we now turn in our search for a better understanding of the significance of sports today.

Sports of the Sky Wanderers

Among the Maya of Mesoamerica,[4] time was the basis for the order and structure of society (Hunt 1996, 76-81). The movements of the sun, moon, planets and stars determined time. Known as Sky Wanderers, these celestial bodies were identified as the deities that gave the gift of time to the Maya. In order to propitiate the Sky Wanderers, and thus ensure the socio-political and architectural structures that they had given were maintained, the Maya believed that sacrifices and rituals were demanded.

Among the Mayan gods were the Twin Heroes, Hunapa and Xbalanque. Hunapa represented the Sun, which was the symbol of life and celestial power. Xbalanque represented the Jaguar, which was the deity of the underworld and death. The myth tells how Hunapa and Xbalanque were born after their fathers, also twins, were invited to Xibalba, or the Mayan place of the dead, to play a ritual ball game with the Lords of the Dead. Their fathers were defeated and decapitated by the Lords of the Dead but, in a grotesque series of events, one of the fathers managed to become the father of the Twin Heroes.

Like their fathers, the Twin Heroes became expert ball players but, unlike their fathers, they defeated the Lords of Death. After sacrificing themselves by fire, the Twins were reborn and returned to Xibalba where they decapitated one another and, to the astonishment of the gods, restored themselves to life. The Death Gods wanted the Twin Heroes to play this trick on them, so Hunapa and Xblanque decapitated two of the Gods, One Death and Seven Death, but left those dead and extracted a promise from the other

Death Gods not to do any more harm. After this, the Twin Heroes became the Sun and Venus, or the Morning and Evening stars, re-enacting their journey each day from Xibalba at dawn and their return there in the evening.

The myth of the Twin Heroes demonstrates the Mayan theme of rebirth through sacrifice. The Mesoamerican ball-court therefore represents the threshold between the human world and the world of Xibalba. The game that was played there was a ritual reenactment of the contest between the Twin Heroes and the Lords of the Dead. It also represented the ordering of time through the movements of the Sun and Venus and the fate of those who were dependent upon this ordering. The interpretations of murals that depict the ball game suggest that the ball was considered to be a symbol of the sun. In effect, the ball court was a cosmological diagram.

The game was played on a paved rectangular court, with smaller perpendicular rectangles at each end. Straight walls ran the length of both sides of the main rectangle. High in the middle of each of these walls were carved stone rings through which a ball could pass. Entwined serpents on the rings suggest the game's origin in the battle with the deities of the underworld. Players wore a heavy belt of wood and leather, kneepads, hip-pads, gloves, and sometimes, even helmets. The game was played at a furious pace, with each team trying to deflect the hard rubber ball through one of the two stone rings, using hips, elbows or knees. At the end of the game, the captain of the losing team was decapitated.

The Mayan ball court at Chichen Itzá on the Yucatán Peninsula includes a relief, in a sequence of sculptures along the base of the walls, showing blood spurting from the neck of a decapitated player as serpents turning into vegetation (Anderson 1996, 47). To the Maya, ritual human sacrifice made rebirth and rejuvenation possible. As the worlds of the living and dead were inextricably linked for the Maya, human bloodletting mirrored the bloodletting of the gods and strengthened the reciprocal relationship between the people and the gods. The reciprocal sacrifice of the gods is evident in the daily descent of the celestial bodies into Xibalba, or death, as well as in the occasional death and rebirth of other deities (Hunt 1996, 81).

The cosmic dimensions of the ballgame were familiar to the Aztecs as well as to the Maya. Both cultures believed that the ball game was taught to humans by the gods, who competed with them (Rosen and McSharry 1992, 145). The Mayan ball game is usually referred to as *Pok-ta-pok* and the Aztec game as *Tlachtli* (Zeigler 1973, 101). When humans played the ball game, they evoked the cosmic confrontation between light and darkness that was represented by the contests between heavenly bodies. Some descriptions of the game highlight the cosmic dimensions of the *tlachos* or ball courts: "*Nahualthachco*, the place of the magical game; *Citlaltlachco*, in the ballgame of the stars; *Teotlachco*, where the gods play ball; *Cuahtlachco*, the ballgame of the rain; and…simply *tlachco*, where…humans compete."

This inextricable association between contest, religion, rebirth and rejuvenation is redolent of the mimetic magic of ancient Olympia. At Dainzú, an archaeological site in southern Mexico, there is evidence that the ball game was played around 300 B. C. (Rosen and McSharry 1992, 151). The sports contests in both Mesoamerica and ancient Greece attempt to promote human survival and welfare by influencing the forces of nature through magical or supernatural means. Yet, while religion remained the primary driving force for these sports, they did come to serve other purposes as well. Betting on ball games in central America was common. The practice appears to have an origin in the mythological wager on the ball game between the human ruler, Huémac, and the rain gods. Some even bet their own bodies. If they lost the wager, they could become slaves or even be sacrificed. The ball game also came to acquire a festival atmosphere. Macuilxochitl, a town near Dainzú, is named after the god of fiestas and ball games. The mimetic or sympathetic magic of ancient Olympic and Mesoamerican competitive sports is evident in the history of sports in many other early societies and civilizations. There are so many striking similarities in relation to the cultic or ritual purposes of sports in societies widely removed by time and space that it is difficult to avoid certain conclusions in relation to their origins. For that reason, it will be helpful to consider some further examples of the religious purposes of early sports.

Sacred Sports

In southern Nigeria, wrestling bouts were practiced as a form of sympathetic magic to promote the growth of crops (Brasch 1989, 2). The Zuñis, a Mexican tribe that lived in an arid zone, first played games to bring rain for their crops. Games were important in winter and early spring to hasten the return of the sun and to ensure a fruitful season. The Wichita tribe of Oklahoma played a game similar to field hockey in which they enacted a symbolic contest between winter and spring to assist the renewal of life and conquer the evil forces of winter. Some Eskimos played seasonal games. In spring, players used a kind of cup and ball to catch the sun. In the autumn, as the sun was moving to the south, a type of cat's cradle was used to trap the sun and slow its departure. The ancient European ball game that eventually became baseball was originally played during the winter solstice. The teams, named Winter and Summer, tried to gain control of the ball or sun, mimicking the battle for life and fertility (Rosen and McSharry 1992, 53).

In general, ball games appear to have enjoyed enormous prominence among the North American Indians and were universal throughout the whole continent (Eisen 1978, 61). The games were played between complementary halves or moieties, towns, and tribes and affected the whole population in some way. The use of moieties indicates that the games had cosmic and religious significance, as will become apparent in the later treatment of the Xavante of Brazil. The physical pursuits and sporting diversions of the North American Indians served other purposes as well and reasons for participation included fitness for war and hunting, recreation, medicine and economics. Contests and gambling were closely associated and were an integral part of medical practices and ceremonial functions. They were also intimately associated with burial ceremonies. The use of games in burial ceremonies brings to mind the funerary games of the ancient Greeks.

Games of chance were prevalent among the North American Indians and served cultural, recreational and economic roles in association with games. There was no monetary system for the exchange of goods and this exchange was the result of the constant exchange of gifts and gambling. Thus, games and gambling become an inextricable part of Indian culture. But gambling is also a sacred ceremony that links Indians to the metaphysics of the cosmos, and acknowledges the power of the trickster and other spirits (Peat 1994, 156). Gambling games embody the significance of flux and the power of the trickster. They bring participants into the deepest processes of the universe, connecting them with their ancestors, who made alliances with the spirits and energies of the universe, and take them back into that world through the great circle of time.

Trickster gods are associated with clown religions and sacred clowns. Clown religions are widely spread throughout the world and are known among the Hopi and Pueblo Indians of North America, associations that will be explored in a later chapter. At this point, however, the association between gambling, games and chance is of most interest. As previously noted, the ancient Greeks thought that winning was an evidence of the favor of the gods and the sacrifices associated with their contests were designed to placate and thus influence the gods in their favor. The similarities between this worldview and that of the North American Indians are marked. Games and gambling in Indian culture are evidently involved in dealing with a capricious universe ruled by capricious gods. Contests among the North American Indians are thus inextricably bound to their conception of the functioning of the cosmos. The same can also be said of certain tribes in South America today.

The Timbira Indians of Brazil engage in a relay race performed by two teams. One team represents the sun; the other, the moon. The race, run on a track that is called the "Milky Way," celebrates the original competition between the sun and moon as they pass through the sky. The ceremonial component of this game is taken as seriously as the competition itself (Rosen and McSharry 1992, 71).

That is also true of the log race of the Xavante of central Brazil. The Xavante believe that the cosmos is made up of opposites and that the fundamental oppositions in human experience, such as life and death, day and night and male and female are part of this cosmic scheme of things. The Xavante construct their society to mirror the cosmos, dividing it into moieties. To avoid contention, people are assigned to different, overlapping pairs of moieties for different purposes (Maybury-Lewis 1992, 148). The purpose of the Xavante log race, which has more to do with ceremony and aesthetics than competition, is to achieve equilibrium and harmony. Each team represents the oppositions that the Xavante believe go to make up the universe. The log race expresses dynamic tension between opposing principles. It seeks to reconcile those opposing principles through alternation, seeking harmony through complementarity.

The religious and cosmic dimensions of contest are also evident in Japan. The earliest recorded sumo contest occurred in the fifth century A. D. and was made as a religious offering. The contest represented divine power. A sumo victory allowed sacred forces to be harnessed to provide a good harvest. For centuries, sumo was associated with an annual agricultural celebration and crop forecast (Sasajima 1988, 58). Even today, sumo includes rites for purification and abolition of evil spirits. Similarly, at a fixed time each year, a hill tribe in Assam, India, arranged a tug-of-war to expel demons. One team represented the forces of evil while the other represented the forces of increase in nature. The result was thought to determine the future (Brasch 1989, 3). The role of early football contests in divination has also been noted (Rosen and McSharry 1992, 57).

These examples reveal the cultic association of contests and games across cultures as widely separated in time and space as ancient Greece and modern Brazil. The relationship they reveal between sports and religion can be seen in many cultures throughout history. The examples could be multiplied greatly. There seems to be something about sports that has particular affinity with religion; but not just any type of religion. The evidence is that sports flourish in religions that seek to placate and influence their gods through mimetic contests, sympathetic magic and associated sacrifices.

Is this mere coincidence or is it possible that there is a common origin and understanding of sports that is expressed in varying ways by different cultures throughout history? There are too many similarities among the diverse cultic purposes of contests and games to support the belief that sports have arisen spontaneously and independently in different cultures throughout history. A common human nature may explain some of the similarities but is inadequate to explain the amazing unity that pervades the cultic purposes of sports across cultures widely separated in time and space.

In 1929, Harold John Massingham suggested that team games originate in dualistic beliefs. Dualism is any theory that holds that there is an irreducible distinction between two different kinds of things in the universe. In the history of religion, dualists are those who hold that God and the devil are coeternal principles. Those who believe that there is an irreducible distinction between good and evil hold a dualist belief. Thus, Massingham is suggesting that team games originated in an attempt to deal with the existence of two irreducible things in the universe. Massingham's theory is seen as interesting but not supported by sufficient data. Yet, if the theory of the dualistic origins of team sports is extrapolated to the broader context of sports in general, there is sufficient evidence to support the belief that sports began in an attempt to reconcile two opposing principles: good and evil. The following section integrates historical data with the Biblical record to produce a theory of the origins of sports that has great explanatory value and major implications for the relationship between Biblical Christianity and sport.

The Dualist Origins of Sports

The fall of mankind introduced a second type of religion to the world. Challenging God's requirements of devotion to good and separation from evil, the fall established the belief on earth that good and evil are fundamental principles of the universe (Steed 1978). There is a great deal of evidence to support the view that sports and games originated in religious practices that are based upon this dualist understanding of the universe. This evidence is most compelling when seen in the context of the impact of dualism upon the course of sacred history. There are significant lessons in this history for Christians and their relationship to sports today, so it is important to begin with a brief history of the fall and its aftermath.

When the eyes of Adam and Eve were opened, they were fearful, defensive, selfish, and aware of their nakedness. They passed these propensities on to their descendents. After Adam and Eve sinned, God implemented the plan of redemption. God proposed to save those who accepted this plan not only by dealing with the guilt and power of sin but also by providing a way to overcome it. God's plan was designed to restore His image in those who were repentant in order that He could safely confer immortality and eternal life upon them (Matthew 5:48; Romans 2:7).

Those who refused this recovery plan became progressively more debased and the contrast between them and those who obeyed God became more marked, until it was necessary within two millennia for God to destroy all who persisted in gross wickedness. Thus, the practical effect of the knowledge of good and evil was the release of a flood of evil. Sin and evil at any level are always dangerous to the order and harmony of the universe. That is why God's plan of redemption encompasses victory over sin in this life. God's true religion throughout history has always required His people to separate from sin. All false religions mingle good and evil or teach salvation in sin.

This latter point is highly significant. It means that Satan has done his most deceptive work within Christianity, for there are many who are expecting to be saved while practicing disobedience to God (Matthew 7:21-29). Satan doesn't care how much good Christians mix with evil as long as sin and evil are tolerated, for he knows that this not only falls short of meeting God's conditions for salvation but also that a little evil is sufficient to corrupt our whole experience. Just one act of disobedience prepared the way for the evils that existed in the late antediluvian world.

Satan seduced Eve into sin by representing the knowledge of good and evil as the path to wonderful knowledge and awe-inspiring experiences. Satan held out the prospect of a life that measured with the life of God. "Ye shall be as gods," he exclaimed, "knowing good and evil." Lies are most deceptive when they contain some truth and so it was with Satan's deception. In the fall, Adam and Eve obtained knowledge of good and evil but it did not make them gods. But the belief that the mingling of good and evil led to fascinating and desirable experiences continued to exercise the distorted imaginations of the Antediluvians, until God cleansed the earth by flood. Those who persisted in rebellion after the flood maintained a belief in this deception and introduced the principle of blending good and evil in their false religions and thus it spread across the world in the great migrations from the Tower of Babel.

The presence of dualist beliefs in religions widely distributed in space and time supports the Biblical testimony that dualism was introduced at the fall and reintroduced to the world before the migrations from the Tower of Babel. The similarities among these religions can be explained by a common origin and the differences can be explained by isolation and the passage of time. The intimate association between sports and dualist beliefs produces a similar result. The common commitment to dualism maintains the ongoing interest in sports while changing circumstances drive the process of adaptation and innovation.

If these conclusions are correct, early sports will contain all the significant elements of the religious mythology that was introduced to the world at the fall. I am using mythology here in the sense of an explanation of the origin of the world and the nature of reality that conflicts with true revelation. Only the Creator God can be a trustworthy source of revelation about the origin and nature of the Creation. God cannot lie. His word is true from the beginning (Psalm 119:160). Thus, anything that contradicts God's revelation is untrue and should be understood as mythology. As the father of lies, Satan is the originator of mythology.

Notice Satan's mythological statement in Genesis 3:4: "And the serpent said unto the woman, Ye shall not surely die." This statement was a direct contradiction of God's revelation to Adam and Eve in Genesis 2:16, 17. The natural immortality of mankind, promoted here by Satan, was a lie but it became the first and most persistent belief among those who continued in rebellion against God after the fall. The spiritist myth that there is an immaterial part of mankind that survives death is almost universally held today.

To reinforce his lie about the natural immortality of mankind and to make it more attractive to Eve, Satan continued his deception in Genesis 3:5, "For God doth know that in the day ye eat thereof, then your eyes shall be opened, and ye shall be as gods, knowing good and evil." Satan held out the dizzying prospect to Eve that she would receive true enlightenment, consisting of the knowledge of good and evil, through initiation into mysteries that were known only to God and which He had unfairly kept from her. This enlightenment was represented as the path to godhood or oneness with God. Oneness with God was to be accomplished through the conjunction and union of good and evil.

Eve's response is recorded in Genesis 3:6: "And when the woman saw that the tree was good for food, and that it was pleasant to the eyes, and a tree to be desired to make one wise, she took of the fruit thereof, and did eat, and gave also unto her husband with her; and he did eat." Eve reasoned that the serpent's words seemed to be consistent with her own observations of the tree, so she took the fruit and ate it. In doing so, Eve distrusted God's revelation and exercised her faculties of observation and reason independently of God. Her choice resulted in the triumph of mythology. And so it is today. Whenever, human reason is placed above God's revelation, the result is descent into myth.

There are three persistent and inextricably linked myths of mankind that were introduced at the fall. The first myth is belief in natural immortality. The second myth is the belief that the union of good and evil is the path to knowledge and godhood. The third myth is the belief that the conjunction of opposites is fundamental to the operation of the universe and is the source of oneness, unity, and harmony. These three myths have led to the amazing diversity of non-Biblical religions that we observe today and throughout human history.

There are many opposites in nature such as light and dark; hot and cold; morning and evening; male and female; and the sun and the moon, which rule the day and night respectively. The creation of these opposites is necessary for life to exist on earth and made great beauty possible (Steed 1978, 21). Their existence gave no endorsement to the need to oppose good with evil, but they were soon linked with good and evil. Those who cast off God as their Protector were forced to promote and defend their own interests. The selfish orientation of their lives led to the invention of deities that would operate in accordance with their mythological beliefs.

The sun and the moon were the most prominent opposites in nature. The sun, being the source of light and heat was considered to be the source of life and was worshipped as the creator. Sun worship became widespread. Often, depictions of the sun in sun-worshipping religions include serpents. Such an illustration from Egypt can be seen in the British museum. The juxtaposition of sun and serpent represents Satan as the creator. At the Temple of Quetzacoatl in Mexico, which is associated with sun worship, the god Quetzacoatl is represented as a feathered serpent. As there are no flying serpents today, this depiction represents a distorted cultural memory of the fall. Winged or feathered serpents are found in early religious practices in places as far apart as Egypt, Rome and Mexico.

The identification of the sun with life led to the introduction of fertility rites and sacrifices in sun-worshipping religions. The union of male and female, so necessary to the propagation of life, led to temple prostitution. Males represented the sun, which was associated with light and good, while females represented the moon, which was associated with darkness and evil. The sympathy that was supposed to exist between these heavenly bodies, including the stars, led to occultism or the belief that heavenly bodies influence the course of human events. Astrological illustrations often show the sun representing maleness and the moon representing femaleness. In medieval astrology, the body was seen as a microcosm of the universe, with the movement and conjunction of the heavenly bodies having a direct effect on human destiny. Fertility rites, human and animal sacrifices and occultism are therefore the inevitable result of embracing dualist beliefs. Significantly, these practices feature repeatedly in the brief review of the association of sports with religion that was undertaken earlier in this chapter. Originally, competitive sports and games were an attempt to influence fertility. Human and animal sacrifices associated with competitive sports were an attempt to placate deities or forces in favor of fertility and prosperity. Sports and games or symbolic contests were seen as a way of influencing human destiny by modifying the influence of the heavenly bodies or forces. Competition in sports also expressed the competitive forces inherent in the fallen human heart. In essence, sports and games began as a mythic attempt to represent and influence the forces of nature and the cosmos and to attain supremacy.

These conclusions bring unity and explanatory power to sports history. Mimesis and sympathetic magic, fertility rites, human and animal sacrifices, symbolic contests and ritual games, the use of moieties for purposes of facilitating harmony and oneness, funeral games, vegetation prizes at the Pan-Hellenic games, rebirth through sacrifice, ball games and sun worship, betting on sports, rites for the purification and abolition of evil spirits, divination, and many other cultic purposes of sports are best understood in terms of a dualist origin for sports. And when these motives are lost through time or secularization, there is still the inherent selfishness of the human heart to drive the modern egocentric preoccupation with competitive sports and games.

Dissonance

The evidence is overwhelming that sports originated in the myths that took root in the ongoing rebellion against God and

His revelation. One of the most powerful reasons to accept the literality of the early Genesis record, aside from the compelling internal evidences, is the explanatory power of the early chapters in relation to the existence and distribution of dualist mythology and the practices that flow from it. With such a clear contrast between God's purposes in Creation as revealed in His word and the distorted, debased view of the universe as portrayed in dualist mythologies and sports, it is simply alarming to discover the extent to which modern Christianity has yielded to the spirit of competitive sports.

Some may object that secularization has purged modern sports of their cultic and distasteful elements and that what remains are the innocent and helpful values of friendly competition and fair play. But can practices that have emerged from rebellion against God and which make no sense outside that context ever be sufficiently sanitized to make them compatible with Christianity? As ancient Greece has exercised the most powerful influence on contemporary Muscular Christianity, it is logical to address this question in the context of the beliefs that undergirded ancient Greek athletics. It will also be helpful to note how the early Christians related to Greek athleticism.

The spirit of competition pervaded ancient Greek education, culture and philosophy as well as athletics and religion. Competition was considered to be as essential to the development of the intellect as it was for the development of the body. Greek myths emphasized the competitive spirit of the gods and heroes. Athletics were regarded as an ideal of the highest order.

The ancient Greek gymnasium combined the functions of sports ground and school. It was usually located in a sacred grove beside a stream. It seems that track events were taught in the gymnasium and jumping and contact sports were taught in the palaestra or wrestling ground. *Gymnos* means to go naked and all training and competition was conducted in a state of nakedness.

Thucydides commented that nakedness was considered by the ancient Greeks to be characteristic of their civilization. Nakedness was also considered to confer heroic status. Yet, whatever the explanation for nakedness, it is glaringly obvious from the visual arts of ancient Greece that homoeroticism is an enduring theme in ancient Greek athletics.

A presiding deity ruled each of the Pan-Hellenic Games. The ancient Olympic Games were sacred and every aspect of the games was invested with sacred significance. Winning was all that mattered in the ancient Olympic Games. Only first prizes were awarded. A victory indicated the favor of the gods. It is this seamless blend of athleticism and religion that gave ancient Greek culture its energy and its sense of cultural superiority.

Today, there is a tendency to see the intimate links between Grecian athleticism and religion as an historical quirk. The modern Olympics, for example, have been described as entirely secular in nature. The perceived value of athletic competition, sports and modern Olympism is no longer expressed in overtly religious terms. Competition is viewed as something inherently valuable and desirable. Thus, the integration of sports and religion in ancient Greece is not seen as a barrier to the enthusiastic use of competitive sports today.

Many who rarely share other beliefs often share this perspective. Evolutionary humanists, who exercise significant influence on physical education and sports policy in the West, can dismiss the relationship between sports and religion in ancient Greece as an evolutionary vestige. Muscular Christians, who are among the most enthusiastic supporters of modern Olympism, see competitive sports as healthy activities that develop character. On this view, the cultic dimensions of ancient Greek sports are quite separate from the values of competitive sports and modern Olympism.

Yet, is it so easy for Muscular Christians today to dismiss the religious and cultic aspects of ancient Greek athleticism? It was the ancient Greek worldview that nourished the competitive instincts of the Greeks and made theirs the most overtly competitive culture in world history. In contrast, the Christian worldview does not contain the elements essential to the development of a competitive culture. The central place of competition in Western society is attributable to our Greek not our Christian heritage. The nineteenth century convergence of Christianity and sports occurred in the context of a major revival of interest in ancient Greece (Harker 1996, 141).

If the religious and cultic dimensions of ancient Greek sports are so easily separated from the essence of competitive sports today, Muscular Christians need to explain why they invest competitive sports with moral significance and why the values of Muscular Christianity are so reminiscent of the athletic values of the ancient Greeks. While the cultic practices of ancient Greek athleticism have disappeared, much of the spirit of these practices survives in the ritual, intensity and excitement of modern sports. The passion for winning remains undiminished.

The spirit of rivalry that infuses sports and Muscular Christianity today is imported from ancient Greece. It is neither derivable from nor compatible with the Biblical worldview. The ancient Olympic Games declined as a result of the rise of Christianity. Notably, thunderous denunciations against Greco-Roman sports appear often in early Christian texts (Poliakoff 1987, 145). However, given the predictions of apostasy in the New Testament, we should not be surprised to find that there were early Christians who thought that the mere presence of athletic metaphors in the New Testament legitimized attendance at pagan athletic spectacles.

There is no research evidence to support the claim that sports build character (Miracle and Rees 1994). In fact, a review of the evidence reveals that the higher the level of involvement in sports, the poorer participants do on measures of sportsmanship. The widespread conflict, cheating and obsessive competitiveness in modern sports is consistent with this evidence. The values of Muscular Christianity are constructed on a flimsy foundation of poor Biblical interpretation, the heroic athletic myths of ancient Greece and the passions of nineteenth century schoolboys and educational elitists. Yet, it is precisely this ideology that is served up to most Christian youth in the name of ministry today. It is time for youth ministry to return to a Biblical foundation.

Notes

[1] British public schools are private institutions.

[2] The Manual Labor movement, popular since the late eighteenth century, provided students with work/study programs, enabling wider access to higher education.

[3] A rhyton is a ceremonial drinking vessel, often in the form of an animal.

[4] Mesoamerica is that part of Mexico and Central America considered civilized when the Spanish arrived in the sixteenth century.

Chapter 2

COSMIC THEATER

Athletes of the Emotions

The most notable thing about the Western theatrical tradition is that it shares the same origin as modern Olympism and sports. Theater and sports emerged from the religious worldview of the ancient Greeks. The same need to placate deities, to promote fertility, to control the forces of nature and to ensure the return of the seasons, which stimulated the origin and development of ancient Greek sports, led to the rituals that evolved into ancient Greek theater. Contemporary theater has its roots in the universal need to give meaning to the workings of the universe.[1]

Drama or tragedy, which originated in the ritual dances to Dionysus, the Greek god of wine and fertility, who died and was reborn in the yearly seasonal cycle, was the first theatrical form to embody the religious worldview of the ancient Greeks. Tragedy developed out of improvisations by the leaders of dithyrambs, hymns sung and danced in honor of Dionysus (Brockett 1987, 18). Dithyrambs probably began as improvised stories that were sung by a choral leader and that included a traditional refrain sung by a chorus. Dithyrambic songs were accompanied by circular dancing around the altar of Dionysus. Dithyrambic dancing was frenzied, miming the joy of the reborn and returning Dionysus (Walter 1973, 66). The Greeks believed that Dionysus possessed dancers when they mimicked him.

Dancers were often dressed as satyrs. In Greek mythology, a satyr was part man and part beast. Satyrs were first represented as uncouth men with a horse's tail and ears and an erect phallus. Later, they were represented as men having a goat's legs and tail. In

Greek, tragedy literally means "goat song" (Brockett 1987, 18). The term tragedy is thought to have originated when the dithyrambic chorus danced for a goat as a prize or around a goat that was then sacrificed. The association of the satyr with the origins of tragedy is of particular interest in that it implies a dualist influence in the origin of theater. The conjunction of opposites as revealed in the mingling of humans and animals in classical mythology represents dualist thinking (Steed 1978, 59).

The choral leader of a dithyramb was a priest of Dionysus. Choral leaders became the first actors in Greek tragedy (Walter 1987, 68). Drama developed rapidly after 534 B.C. when Athens instituted a contest for the best tragedy presented at the City Dionysia. Shortly after this time, dramatists were required to supply a satyr play each time they competed at the City Dionysia. A satyr play was a burlesque comedy performed after a classical tragic trilogy, taking its name from the chorus of half-human, half-beast companions of Dionysus. A satyr play frequently involved a legendary hero from the previous trilogy who was joined by eleven cowardly, lecherous and wine-loving satyrs, led by Silenus, the foster father of Dionysus, in a parody of a myth. The boisterous action took place in a rural setting and involved vigorous dancing and indecent language and gesture.

Comedy was the last of the major dramatic forms to receive official recognition at the City Dionysia, achieving this in 487-486 B.C. Aristotle wrote that comedy developed out of the improvisations of the leaders of phallic songs. Fantastic exaggerations served to lampoon real life. In addition to fantasy, farce, involving such subjects as eating, drinking, sex, wealth and leisure, was typical. Comedies included some of the most beautiful lyrics and most obscene passages in Greek literature. Comedy was consistent with the Greek view of their gods. They believed their gods to be sublimely beautiful, ageless, sinister and terrifying but also hilariously funny (Levi and Porter 1988, 22).

Old comedy gradually took on a six-part structure: the introduction in which the fantasy is explained and developed; the entry of the chorus; the contest or ritualized debate between opposing principals; the audience addressed by the chorus, in which scurrilous criticism was hurled at prominent citizens; a series of farcical scenes; and a final banquet or wedding. The final scene or *komos* usually concludes with the reconciliation of the characters and their exit to a feast (Brockett 1987, 24). Members of the chorus were disguised in animal masks while the players were dressed in phallic costumes (Huizinga 1955, 144). The highly formal structure of comedy is thought to derive from ancient fertility rites.

Another possible source of influence on Athenian comedy is the mime, which supposedly made its appearance at Megara near Athens shortly after 581 B.C. While no mimes from this period have survived, later mimes are short satirical treatments of domestic situations or are parodies of myths. It may be that the Athenians incorporated mimic scenes with their own phallic choruses. Mime involved such forms as playlets, mimetic dance, imitation of animals and birds, acrobatics and juggling.

In a remarkable synthesis of the common spirit and origins of ancient Greek theater and sports, Antonin Arnaud, the theatrical theorist and innovator, thought of the actor as "an athlete of the emotions" (Rosen and McSharry 1992, 58). Aristotle believed that imitation or mimesis aroused the sentiments that are imitated (Huizinga 1955, 162). Both ancient Greek athletics and sports shared a devotion to mimesis. Athletic mimesis was associated with the promotion of fertility. Theatrical mimesis was designed to bring back Dionysus, the male god of fertility.

Similarly, both sports and theater were agonistic or competitive. Sports competition mirrored the Greek view of the universe. Greek gods were fiercely competitive. Just as athletes sought to win glory for themselves, dramatists and poets competed for theatrical laurels. Greek drama, like Greek athletics, produced winners and losers. The agonistic aspect of the theater was also reflected in the content and presentation of drama and comedy. Conflict and debate were institutionalized in these dramatic forms, both on stage and also between those on the stage and the audience. The public shared the tension of the conflict like a crowd at an athletic contest (Huizinga 1955, 145).

Conflict, which was the source of both dramatic tension and comic relief in Greek theater, did not necessarily need to end unhappily. The conflict between such opposite elements as good and evil could lead to comprehension and reconciliation (Hartnoll 1995, 9). The motif of good and evil in medieval morality plays echoes this resolution. The reconciliation of opposites in Greek theater alludes to a dualistic influence in the origins of Greek theater. In classical mythology, the balancing of opposites can be used to achieve a desirable non-dual state. Thus, competition can be seen as essential to athletic and theatrical mimesis. Both attempt to influence cosmic events.

The concept of the mingling of opposites may help to explain the unity of tragedy and comedy in Greek theater. Huizinga (1955, 145) draws our attention to Plato's *Symposium*, in which Socrates says that the true poet must be at once both tragic and comic and that the whole of life must be felt as a blend of tragedy and comedy. Comedy emerged out of tragedy and is, at one level, opposite to it. Yet, comedy deals with the same issues as drama, only from an opposite approach. The treatment of issues from opposite perspectives may be seen as just another way of facilitating their reconciliation.

The emotional harmony between athletics and sports is also probable at the religious level. Mandell suggests that it is likely that many athletes, after pleading for celestial assistance, competed in a religious trance (Mandell 1976, 13). This suggestion is supported by the mood in which drama was performed. Dionysian ecstasy and dithyrambic rapture captivated the players. Masks worn by players helped them to withdraw from the ordinary world and to be transformed into another ego, which was not so much represented as incarnated and actualized. Players drew the audience into the same state of mind.

The extant tragedies and comedies of Greek theater reveal a fascination for the sordid aspects of life. Yet, Western theater continues to draw inspiration from these plays. Contemporary drama thrives on the same issues of fate, meaning, authority, violence, good and evil, the human psyche, and everyday life that engaged the early Greek dramatists. The Greek preoccupation with heroic themes, sex and relationships is clearly evident in modern drama. Comedy remains, for the most part, bawdy, satirical and anti-authority.[2]

The persistence of Greek characteristics in modern theater parallels the ongoing inspiration that Western sports derive from ancient Greece, creating many of the same difficulties for Christians. The meaning and purpose of something today is bound up with its origins. Theater is uniquely the invention of Greek religion. Without the peculiar elements of the Greek worldview, theater could not have emerged. Tragedy, even when it had outgrown Dionysian ritual, retained the closest ties with religion and maintained its religious qualities (Finley 1977, 101). The Greek conception of their myths, their gods and the cosmos provided the recurring themes of Greek theater. In contrast, Judeo-Christianity lacked the essential elements for the development of theater, as it lacked the elements necessary for the development of sports.

Many Christians today justify the adoption of theatrical forms in the churches on the basis that these forms update methods of ministry, worship and evangelism and make them more relevant to the contemporary world. It is true that relevance has its place. We should not set out to be unnecessarily irrelevant or quaint. Paul was willing to adapt himself to the cultural circumstances of the people he was trying to reach (1 Corinthians 9:22). But Paul also understood that what was lawful for him to do in these circumstances was limited by the will of God (1 Corinthians 6:9, 10, 12). The concept of relevance is defined and enclosed by the principles laid down in the Bible.

In the context of sacred history, it is ironic that the argument for the adoption of theatrical forms today on the basis of relevance should be advanced at all. The world into which Jesus was born included a Roman presence. The Romans had adopted and transformed Greek theatrical forms and practices in the third century B.C. (Brockett 1987, 54). The Romans officials and troops in Palestine would therefore have been familiar with a variety of theatrical forms. There was a theater at Caesarea, so it is likely that traveling troupes of actors and mimes visited Palestine to entertain the Romans.

Theater was culturally relevant for these Roman expatriates. Yet, when Jesus came in contact with Romans and ministered to them, He did not alter His approach significantly. He attempted to reach all classes and nationalities through teaching, preaching and healing. Jesus taught His disciples to do the same. Although the Romans that Jesus encountered were separated from Him more widely in religion and background than are most Christians and secularists in the West today, Jesus avoided theatrical forms in bringing the gospel to them.

Roman theater was almost always associated with festivals, most of them religious. It might be argued that this is the reason why Jesus chose not to use theatrical forms in communicating the gospel to the Romans. No doubt this was a major reason for Jesus' choice. Yet, by the time of Jesus, the theatrical content of the festivals that honored the gods mattered less than the fact that the entertainments were offered. Jesus obviously chose not to present his message theatrically because, aside from its pagan associations, theater was an inappropriate way to represent and communicate the gospel. The early Christians followed Jesus' example.

Opposition from the early church was one of the reasons for the decline of the Roman theater that began in the fourth century A.D. (Brockett 1987, 83). That opposition stemmed from the paganism of the festivals, which incorporated theater, the licentiousness of the mimes and the ridicule that the mimes heaped upon Christian practices. Even as the church began to compromise with paganism after the political conversion of the Roman Empire, it retained a sense of the dangers of pagan theater. The fifth council of Carthage in 401 A.D. decreed excommunication for anyone who attended the theater rather than church on holy days. In 692 A.D. the Trullan Synod, convened by the Byzantine emperor, Justinian II, attempted to have all mimes and theatrical performances banned (Brockett 1987, 91).

Ironically, after the decline in the fortunes of the theater that accompanied the rise of Christianity and the disintegration of the Roman Empire, theater was reborn in the liturgical drama of the Roman Catholic Church. The Roman church, in seeking to extend its influence, often adopted pagan and folk festivals, many of which had theatrical elements. By the tenth century, possibilities for dramatic presentation were provided by most church services. With its antiphonal or responsive songs, the mass is not unlike a drama. Certain religious holidays were celebrated with theatrical activities such as processions. From the tenth to the twelfth centuries, liturgical drama began to incorporate mystery and miracle plays.

While the medieval church encouraged early liturgical drama because of its didactic or teaching qualities, the focus shifted to entertainment and spectacle, causing the church to remove drama from the church building to the town market square. The plays retained their religious and moral focus but presentation was increasingly secularized, the result being the development of morality plays in the fifteenth century. The morality plays incorporated allegorical characters, comic tension, movement and songs in folk plays, secular farces and pastoral dramas. Morality plays had many similarities with Greek comedy. The general illiteracy of the Dark and Middle Ages was fertile ground for such plays.

The unavoidable conclusion to be drawn from this history is that the medieval theater, the forerunner of modern theater and the link between classical and modern theater, was born in the great falling away of the doctrinal integrity, learning and piety of the Roman Catholic Church during the dark centuries following its accession to religious and cultural dominance in Europe. Significantly, the development of medieval theater followed a similar pattern to that of theater in ancient Greece. Greek tragedy, with its emphasis on the great issues of fate, gave rise to comedy. Similarly, the mystery and miracle plays, with their emphasis on human salvation, gave rise to the comic and farcical forms of morality plays. Little wonder, then, that when the authority of the Bible was restored in the Protestant Reformation, it put an end to most religious drama in Northern Europe by the middle of the sixteenth century.

Therefore, the contemporary Protestant claim that theatrical forms are necessary and relevant to Christian worship, nurture and witness, especially among the young, lacks credible Biblical support and defensible historical precedent. It hardly seems coincidental that the adoption of theatrical forms in Protestantism, which occurred in the late twentieth century, was coextensive with the rise of ecumenism. The declining emphasis on doctrinal distinctiveness that inevitably accompanies the ecumenical spirit is friendly to the revival of medieval dogma and perspectives.

Carroll (1993) argues that the failure of humanism to conquer death or establish a sense of community has left a deep spiritual void in the West that can only be filled by returning to the values and spirit of the Counter-Reformation. Some historians are even discarding the term "Reformation" as misleading (Fernández-Armesto and Wilson 1996, 9). The current trend in Reformation historiography is to view the religious ferment of the sixteenth and seventeenth centuries as an age of "transition" in which a common theme and purpose spanned hostile groups.

The failure of modernism to nourish the soul has also left a cultural void. The collapse of reason as a guiding principle in human affairs has engendered a hunger for the cosmic certainties of the past. Yet, the hunger is not for a Protestant past but a Catholic one. As Frayling (1995, 7) points out in relation to popular culture, the Middle Ages are alive and well today. In books, movies and philosophy, the medieval vision is returning. Ecumenism has done much to restore this vision by legitimizing Catholicism and by highlighting the decline of distinctive Protestant beliefs and cultural values. Hence, the adoption of medieval theatrical forms in Protestantism is simply further evidence of the exhaustion of Protestant vitality and the contemporary ascendancy of Roman Catholicism.

A noticeable characteristic of the scripts available on Christian web sites is the lack of doctrinal and denominational distinctiveness. Yet, the bland ecumenism is not generally matched by any sensitivity to good taste. Many of the scripts available are more closely attuned to Greek comedy than they are to the lofty and dignified themes of Christianity. Whimsical titles, exaggerated characters with comic names, ridiculous themes and degenerate settings, and coarse language are common in scripts. I have even encountered expletives. In contrast, when Bible writers deal with the reality of sin and evil, they are never vulgar or base.

The true spirit of the theatrical forms that have been adopted in Protestantism is betrayed by the parallel emergence of competitions for writers and performers. Competition is characteristic of the Greek heritage in Western civilization. It has nothing to do with Christianity. Competition destroys the oneness of mind that is to characterize Christians. Competition works directly against the spirit of Christianity. It thrives on vainglory or selfish ambition and conceit. Competitions for Christian writers and performers indicate the extent to which the spirit of ancient Greece dominates the modern Christian consciousness. The theatrical scene in contemporary Protestantism is fraught with danger as the following discussion reveals.

The beast that rises up out of the sea in Revelation 13, which speaks blasphemies and wars against the saints of God, and which accepts illicit worship in the great final crisis at the end of the world, is mostly leopard. The beast is a composite of the world prophetic kingdoms of the seventh chapter of Daniel, thus representing the religious, philosophical and cultural heritage of these kingdoms. The leopard beast is the third world kingdom after Babylon and Medo-Persia. It represents Greece, as it also does in Nebuchadnezzar's image in the second chapter of Daniel. Babylon is the first kingdom. It was replaced by Medo-Persia and in turn by Greece. The fact that the composite beast of Revelation 13 is mostly leopard indicates that the cultural heritage of ancient Greece, its most seductive legacy to the world, will be everywhere evident in the last days.

But everything opposed to God will pass away when Jesus comes. In Daniel 2, Nebuchadnezzar's image is destroyed. In Daniel 7, the little horn is judged and his dominion taken away. The beast and the false prophet of Revelation 13 are destroyed together. The widespread intrusion of Greek theatrical forms into contemporary Protestantism is compelling evidence that the final crisis of Revelation 13 is almost upon us. Those Christians who embrace the theatrical heritage of ancient Greece in the last days are in a state of deception. By imbibing the spirit of paganism and operating on false principles, they will be powerless to gain the victory over the beast, his image, his mark and the number of his name.

Greek theatrical forms obscure God's character and frustrate the restoration of God's image in His people. They are not suitable vehicles for worship or for communicating the gospel. Their presence in the churches is an indication that Protestantism is being brought to crisis. The dimensions of this looming crisis can best be understood in terms of the reasons why the theatrical forms that have been adopted in contemporary Protestantism are unsuitable for Christian use. The remainder of this chapter is devoted to revealing these reasons.

Drama

In the centuries preceding the emergence of drama, the rituals and celebrations involved in the worship of Dionysus were of a particularly nauseating kind. Dionysus was considered to be the son of Zeus and a mortal named Semele. He was reared by satyrs and killed, cut into pieces and resurrected (Brockett 1987, 19). Dionysus was associated with wine, revelry and fertility and the early rites associated with his celebration and worship were ecstatic in nature and often involved drunkenness, sexual orgies, and the rending and devouring of animal and human victims. The resurrection theme in the Dionysian rites is a satanic counterfeit of the historical resurrection of Jesus Christ. Drama emerged from this counterfeit religion, making it a bizarrely inappropriate medium to use in Christian worship and evangelism today.

Furthermore, there is a principle in the Bible that requires the sacred to be kept apart from the profane (Leviticus 10:10). In relation to the house of worship, God desires that it be used only for holy purposes. Greek drama was performed in sacred precincts. Early theaters were always built near a temple. An altar was placed at the centre of the *orchestra* or dancing place, where drama was performed. The contemporary stage is a derivative of the 'sacred' spaces of Greek theater that were designed to act out the hideous myths of Dionysus. Consequently, it is wrong to set up a stage for drama in a sanctuary dedicated to Christian worship.

God is also particular about the manner in which He is worshipped. From the beginning, God has prescribed how He is to be worshipped. God does not change. The typical ceremonies of the Old Testament sanctuary may no longer be in force, but the principles of worship remain the same. Worship should be offered in a manner that befits the Creator of the universe (Psalm 95:6). It should draw attention to God and give glory to Him. In contrast, drama focuses attention on the actors. The thirst for applause that motivates actors is not the spirit that can bring glory to God. Anything that draws attention to the human element in worship should be avoided.

Some Christians believe that anything offered to God in sincerity is acceptable to Him. But God does not accept everything done in His name. Actors may believe that they are offering God worship but true worship is bound up in obedience to God (1 Samuel 15:22). We have been warned that there will be those in the last days who will have a form of godliness but who will deny the power of Christianity. Those who do this will turn from the truth to embrace fables or myths (2 Timothy 4:4). The current enthusiasm for drama in worship fulfils this prediction.

God's word is the active agent in worship and evangelism. It is the source of true knowledge and understanding. God uses the preaching of His word to instruct His people and to reach the ungodly. He reaches the hearts of men by first engaging their reason. On the other hand, drama appeals to the emotions. As a result, when the excitement and the spectacle of drama is over, the word of God has not been fixed firmly in the mind. Routine exposure to drama will encourage an emotional religion that is not firmly grounded in God's word. In fact, it may actively discourage a taste for the Bible or condition people not to react to its claims.

Modern theatrical drama is profoundly opposed to the Biblical worldview and the mind of Christ. In harmony with its sordid origins, drama continues to excite passion and glorify vice. Its use by Christians diminishes the glorious gospel of Jesus Christ and builds bridges to a world of temptations that God would spare His people. Drama encourages a love of display that is at odds with the humility that should clothe the mind of the Christian. It involves unnecessary expense and consumes time and energy that ought to be devoted to more worthy ends.

Drama in worship or evangelism is submission to the spirit of the age. Forms of worship are changed to accommodate religion to human wants. But the Bible makes no concession to selfish human wants, speaking instead to our real needs. The idea that Christians should conform to worldly practices in order to facilitate the acceptance of Christianity became popular in the fourth century Roman church. Consequently, a flood of pagan customs, practices and idolatry poured into the church, making it barely distinguishable from paganism. The experiment was a total failure and it is alarming to discover the extent to which such a Biblically and historically discredited idea should be promoted today as some marvelous new light or the leading of the Holy Spirit.

Dance

Today, drama in worship is often accompanied by dance. However, dance provides another clear contrast between the pagan worship of ancient Greece and Judeo-Christian worship practices. Certain types of dancing are known in Scripture. Israelite women danced to celebrate a military victory. Dancing also occurred during social celebrations at Israelite religious festivals or events, at family reunions and on secular occasions. Yet, only four Scriptural references refer without dispute to religious dancing and none of these is associated with public worship in the House of God (Bacchiocchi 2000, 222). No dancing is recorded as taking place in the Temple, synagogue or early church. Neither is it associated with evangelism anywhere in Scripture.

David danced before the Lord on the joyful national and religious occasion that the ark was brought to Jerusalem. Yet, David's dance was not done in the context of a regular worship service and there is no evidence that David's dance on this occasion was ever viewed by the Israelites as a precedent for dancing during worship services. David gave extensive instructions to the Levites on the nature of the musical ministry that was to take place in the Temple, carefully defining what was acceptable and what was not acceptable, but no such instructions are given in relation to dance. If David chose to distinguish between sacred and secular musical forms in relation to Temple worship, this omission is significant. If dancing were acceptable in the Temple, surely David would have distinguished between acceptable and unacceptable forms of accompanying music.

Similarly, the references to dance in Psalm 149:3 and Psalm 150:4 do not provide unequivocal evidence that dance is an acceptable part of public worship. The term "dance" in these two verses is disputed, some scholars believing that the Hebrew word translated "dance" is a possible allusion to a pipe instrument, as is provided in the marginal reading of both verses in the King James Version (Bacchiocchi 2000, 223). The two verses also appear in the context of figurative language. For example, God's people cannot praise Him "in his mighty firmament" (Psalm 150:2) because they live on earth and not in heaven. The purpose of the psalm is to invite everything that breathes or makes a sound to praise the Lord everywhere, not to specify the location, the musical instruments and the activities to be included in praise for church worship.

The absence of dance in the formal worship of the Israelites stands in stark contrast to the heathen practices of the time. When the Israelites apostatized at Sinai, they danced around the golden calf. At Carmel, the prophets of Baal included dance in the invocation of their gods. The Greeks invoked the blessings of their gods and worshipped through dance. They also ensured crop fertility through the sympathetic magic of dance (Walter 1973, 63). Cosmic dances, which depicted planetary movements, were performed in honor of Urania, the dance Muse and the patroness of astronomy. The Muse, Tersichore, achieved ecstasy through dance.

Ecstasy was associated with many ancient Greek dances. At the festivals of Anthesteria and Aiora, young girls were swung to ensure high or good crops. Dancers became possessed during these fertility rites and prophesied success or failure of the crop. The dances were mimetic in that their purpose was for like to produce like. Dancers were possessed and became one with the god being invoked.

Dance was associated with mimes and was adapted to comedy. The kordax was a comic dance style that was distinguished by its lewdness. Like drama, dance represented the Greek view of their gods. Comic dance was compatible with the Greek worldview. Jewish dancing, on the other hand, was always constrained by the Jewish understanding of the great dignity and purity of God. The dancing of the Jews could be exuberant but it was never sensuous or suggestive. It expressed joyful emotions within the bounds of restraint and reason. The Old Testament never recognizes dance as one of the elements of worship to be used in formal, corporate worship. The word of God was central in religious gatherings (Ezekiel 33:30-33).

The ecstatic element in the dances of many cultures throughout history may be one of the reasons why God did not permit dancing in formal worship. Certainly, there are many remnants of shamanism and ecstatic possession evident in dances in non-Christian religions today. Recently, a movement has developed in contemporary environmentalism called bioregionalism, which proposes that humans attune their needs and lifestyles to the region in which they live. Bioregionalism included the notion that humans should adopt, amongst other things, the religious liturgies, dance and music that are unique to the region they inhabit (Berry 1988, 168). In numerous cases this would involve participation in animist and spiritist dances and rituals. For these reasons,

Christians would be wise to maintain the rejection of liturgical dance that most Protestant denominations have maintained until recently. Unambiguous Scriptural evidence should be demanded of all who seek to introduce dance into worship or evangelism.

Tragicomedy

The emergence of comedy from tragedy in the early classical period of ancient Greece owes much to the dualism of the archaic period that preceded it. The whole conceptual and imaginative world of the archaic Greeks was profoundly dualistic (Huizinga 1955, 53). Comedy as a counterpoint to tragedy fits readily into a world in which the tribal structure and the mental world inhabited by the opposing halves of the tribe could not only contain room for contest and rivalry but also for reciprocal help. For the ancient Greeks, comedy and tragedy are consistent with the dualism that saturates the cosmos. Hence, comedy achieves its significance not only in providing a contrast to tragedy but also in its active participation in the world of meaning that generated it. In this sense, the meaning of comedy arises from its dissimilar but complementary treatment of the dramatic elements of the ancient Greek worldview.

Comedy is based upon a dualistic view of man, in which bodily instinct is mixed incongruously with rational intellect, producing an ironic view of human behavior. Satire works ironically by highlighting the difference between profession of virtue and actual behavior. Comedy works best where the difference is greatest between profession and performance. That is why the subject matter of comedy is usually the contradictions in those things that are closest to humans and that are taken most seriously by them. Comedy is a dimension of the serious. That explains why the greatest of the comic figures seem to project an air of pathos—a sense of loneliness and vulnerability in a capricious universe. Comedy inhabits the realm of tragicomedy.

The serious dimension of comedy belies the perception that many Christians have that comedy exists in a dimension of fun, where everyday realities are suspended. A similar misperception occurs in relation to competition in sports. It is presumed that competition in sports exists in a play dimension outside the normal constraints of everyday life. Hence, biting satire and aggressive competitiveness are tolerated and enjoyed in comedy and sports as socially acceptable fun, and even productive of good, when similar activities not constrained by rules and conventions would be viewed as hurtful and destructive. But something does not cease to be destructive just because it is placed in the wrong category.

Comedy and the comical thrive by mocking beliefs, people and institutions and they inevitably diminish that which they mock. Comedy introduces people to a world of the imagination in which nothing is sacred. Comedy breaks down the boundaries between the sacred and the common and makes strivings for rectitude seems silly and quixotic. The world of comedy is a cynical world. It brings everything down to the lowest common denominator and takes the mind captive.

I know from personal experience that this is true. In my late adolescence, I cultivated a taste for comic and curious verse. I found my mind running habitually in a light and frivolous vein. This coincided with a period of my life in which I found it difficult to apply myself to study or the serious realities of life. Today, I try to avoid the frivolous and the comical elements of popular culture, as they can destroy my connection with Christ faster than almost anything else. Comedy and the comical destroy appreciation for the true inner piety of the Christian life and destroy the serious impressions that God would make upon us through the preaching of His word. A particularly destructive form of the comic imagination in contemporary Christianity is the satirical cartoon, which seems to be given a prominent places in many magazines.

Comedy is the antithesis of the spirit of Jesus Christ. Preachers who use comical illustrations or jokes destroy the force of their preaching. The jokes and the asides will be remembered long after the lofty sentiments have been forgotten. That is why Jesus never resorted to comedy or witticisms to get His message across. He knew that the human mind runs more readily to the dishonorable than to the honorable. His ministry was characterized by attempts to bring the mind to the contemplation of eternal realities. There is no record in the New Testament that Jesus deliberately sought to create laughter in his discourses. His example is to be followed by all Christians. He also showed that we may be sociable and enjoy the fellowship of others without detriment to spirituality.

Consequently, it is deep spiritual blindness that can see merit in the use of clowning and cognate activities like mime in Christian witness. Paul indicated that Christians are ambassadors for Christ. An ambassador represents the interests of his government, in this case the government of heaven, in a manner consistent with the dignity of his or her office. Clowns are identified with the coarse jest, the spirit of frivolity and satirical and disorderly behavior. No earthly ambassador would demean his country by representing it in the trappings of a clown. Christians have been called with a "holy calling" (2 Timothy 1:9). How careful we should be to represent Jesus appropriately.

The category of the comic, to which the clown belongs, is closely connected with folly in the highest and lowest sense of the word (Huizinga 1955, 6). In the highest sense of the word, folly is the antithesis of wisdom just as darkness is the antithesis of light (Ecclesiastes 2:13). At the level of ideas, it is folly to connect clowning with wisdom. In the lowest sense of the word, folly is about foolish and unbecoming behavior. As the epitome of foolish behavior, clowning embodies the lower as well as the higher sense of folly, making it impossible for clowning to represent the wisdom that proceeds from God.

The attempted fusion of polar opposites such as good and

evil, and light and darkness, is not the wisdom of heaven. In fact, Scripture pronounces a woe on all who call evil good and good evil and who put darkness for light and light for darkness (Isaiah 5:20). The woe extends to those who are wise in their own eyes. Despite the undeniable link between clowning and folly, there are those who promote clowning as a spiritual gift and as a calling from God. But the Holy Spirit is not divided against Himself (Matthew 12: 25). As Scripture warns, "There is a way that seemeth right unto a man, but the end thereof are the ways of death" (Proverbs 16:25).

The gospel is no less sacred because it is to be communicated to children and youth. A clown can no more aptly represent Jesus to this group than to adults. First impressions are very powerful impressions and young people who are introduced to Christianity through clowning are hardly likely to catch a vision of its true sacredness. The earliest ancestors of the clown flourished in ancient Greece and Rome. The bawdy and satirical persona of the clown in ancient times remains alive and well in the circus clown today. Clowning has not outgrown its impure origins for clowns are still categorized with illusionists, puppeteers, comedians, jugglers, fire-eaters, dancers, and mime, mask and stunt artists.

The use of a symbol that is associated today with the circus and the popular entertainment industry is made even more injudicious by the existence of 'sacred' clowns today. A sacred clown is a "ritual or ceremonial figure, in various preliterate and ancient cultures throughout the world, who represents a reversal of the normal order." In some traditions, clowning has an apotropaic role or a role in averting evil. The Koyemshi or dancing clowns of the Pueblo Indians engage in obscene and sacrilegious actions during important religious ceremonies as a means of highlighting the underworld and for reasons of social control. Hopi clowns fulfill a similar role (Maybury-Lewis 1992, 213). It is considered that they are endowed with supernatural powers, enabling them to get away with things forbidden to others.

A Hopi scholar and clown, Emory Sekaquaptewa, explains that Hopi clowns "show us the futility of believing that we can be perfect, correct or confident of ourselves" (Maybury-Lewis 1992, 213). Hopi clowns behave scandalously to make us think about morality. In essence, that is the adopted role of clowning in Christianity. Sadly, clowning in Christianity today links the religion of the Bible with clown religions, medieval morality plays and the buffoonery of ancient Greek and Roman comedy.

The contemporary clown is not a neutral or harmless symbol. Indeed, clowns have never been neutral figures. Germanic and Celtic myths are full of clown figures, representing grotesque deities (Campbell and Moyers 1988, 219). The Nigerians worshipped a trickster god. Until recently, Christians who adhere to the authority of the Bible have taken a lead in loosening the hold of paganism and myth wherever they have found it. The early Christians shunned the comic theater of the Greco-Roman world and sought to destroy its influence. The Reformation undermined the influence of medieval morality plays. In recent centuries, Protestant missionaries have weakened the grip of mythology in many parts of the world. Yet, today, many Christians are embracing the very symbols that deny this heritage and that mock the deepest spiritual and emotional needs of youth.

Masks, Mimes, Marionettes and Magicians

The adoption of drama, dance and comedy by the churches has brought with it a number of activities that have abominable histories and contemporary associations. Masks originated in religious rituals and have been used in many cultures throughout history. In ancient Greece, masks were used in tragedy and comedy. Masks disguise the wearer and usually convey an alternative identity. Masks portrayed gods, mythological beings, spirits, animals and other beings believed to exercise power over humans. Masks were used in fertility and war rituals and by shamans. Masked dancers were frequently believed to be transformed into or possessed by the spirit inhabiting or represented by the mask. Notably, masks were used in medieval mystery and miracle plays. Today, masks are still used in many cultures for ritual purposes. They retain their unholy associations and should be shunned by all Christians.

Mime has its origins in mimetic rituals. In ancient Greece, mime covered playlets, mimetic dance, imitation of animals and birds, singing, acrobatics and juggling (Brockett 1987, 52). Mimes were probably the first professional entertainers. In Rome, mime seemed to designate almost any type of entertainment offered in the theater. It was in Rome that mime reached its lowest point. The death of criminals in the Coliseum was incorporated into mime, the actors experiencing the suffering and death of the characters they represented (Olivová 1984, 180). On other occasions, criminals dressed as actors in priceless tunics were set alight and died as part of the climax to proceedings. The costume was known as the *tunica molesta* — the "troublesome tunic." In the fifth century, mime had become so debased that all mimes were excommunicated.

Today, mime preserves the only dramatic continuity between the classical world and modern Europe. However, its meaning is more restricted than in ancient Rome. It now refers to mimetic gesture and dance, usually silent, and either tragic or comic, in which the mime seeks to provide entertainment through narrative. Mimes dress in black with contrasting white makeup or masks. Mimes can be encountered in the theater, at festivals or in the streets. Mime has been appropriated as a vehicle for the transmission of the Christian gospel. Yet, mimetic dance continues to be part of many non-Christian cultures throughout the world, many of which are animistic or spiritualistic in nature. The ongoing association of mime with Spiritism makes it an unfortunate choice for Christians who wish to convey the light of the glorious gospel of Christ.

Puppets and marionettes are inanimate figures used in the

theater to represent humans, animals or mythological persons. Puppets are usually operated by hand whereas marionettes are typically operated by strings or wires from above. In the eighteenth and nineteenth centuries, puppets and marionettes were used to perform most forms of Western drama. Puppet figures, such as Punch and Judy, were particularly noted for slapstick comedy, violence, and exaggeration.

A recent archaeological find in northern Peru reveals a rather dreadful association of puppets and religion. A set of life-size dancing skeleton puppets, made out of real bones, were found buried beneath the floor of a Moche temple (Keys 1999, 231). Examination of the bones indicated that they had been defleshed with butchering instruments and kept in an articulated state. As the culture was likely to have been shamanistic in nature, it is probable that the puppets were used in rituals or ceremonies for contacting the dead. They may have symbolized the ancestors whose intercession would have been sought in times of crisis. Such a discovery hardly suggests puppets and marionettes are a harmless vehicle for conveying divine truth.

The magical arts have been known since ancient times and were condemned by God in the Old Testament (Deuteronomy 18:10-12). In New Testament times, magic began to decline under the influence of Christianity. Sorceries and enchantments were an abomination to God because they were involved in communication with evil spirits. God gave Paul special miracles to show that the power of God was stronger than the power of the spirits in Ephesus (Acts 19:1-20). Paul admonished the Ephesians not to have anything to do with the unfruitful works of darkness (Ephesians 5:11).

Despite this, there are Christians today who describe themselves as "Christian magicians." These magicians are illusionists or conjurers who seek to use their skills in witness. They reject the occult connotations of magic but see nothing wrong in creating illusions and using deception to communicate the gospel. Their argument is that they are magicians in the harmless sense of the term. However, deception in any form is an insidious evil and is never harmless. Satan seduced Eve into sin through the deceptive arts and those who use these arts today open themselves up to supernatural forces and create a bridge for the unwary to a world inhabited by evil spirits. Through the practice of illusionism and conjuring, Satan is able to gain access to minds that have become confused and disoriented.

It is significant that deception in sports is one of the chief ways to confuse an opponent and to put him or her off balance. Boxers feint and try to deceive their opponents. Footballers throw dummy passes and try to mask their real intentions in running plays. Baseball, basketball, cricket and tennis and numerous other sports thrive on deception. When an opponent is confused, he or she is put in a position of disadvantage. Where deception is practiced, people are on enchanted ground. Practices that are not as open as the day originate with the prince of darkness.

The Mirror of the Cosmos

Theater originated in the mirror of the imagination that the ancient Greeks held up to the cosmos. They saw in this mirror the capricious gods who govern the affairs of nature and of man. Lying behind these gods they perceived the great issues of fate and destiny. The Greeks gave to theater the sense of tragedy and tragicomedy that this combination engendered in their minds. Discerning Jews and Christians understood that the Greek and Roman theaters embodied a worldview that was completely at odds with their own. Likewise, the Reformers understood the need to avoid the religious drama and comedy that had developed in the medieval church. Sadly, these perspectives are largely viewed today as outdated or outmoded vestiges of a Christianity that is no longer relevant to the modern world.

But just how effective is theater as a medium of conveying truth? Even in ancient Greece, there were critics of the writers and performers of tragedy. Socrates, for example, understood that the makers of tragedy were not only imitators of the gods but were also to a significant extent the makers of the gods (Plato's *Republic*, Book X). Their representations were generative, in the sense that they had no models in the visible universe. They were interpreting that part of the universe that had no analogue in human experience. Socrates criticized tragic poetry for the kind of knowledge that it generated through imitation. He felt that imitation led to an inferior type of knowledge. The imitator knows nothing of what is but rather what looks like it *is*. The maker or user of something in the visible world has knowledge of that thing but the imitator is concerned with something that is third from the truth about that object.

Socrates is dealing with the deficiencies of the tragic poetry that preceded him and his criticisms include the poets of tragic theater. He judges that the knowledge conveyed by the tragedian writer is inferior. He also draws attention to the way in which stage imitation distorts things, likening the knowledge conveyed by puppeteering and other things of the kind to wizardry. He felt that these things created confusion in the soul. It is not difficult to see Socrates' reasoning. The knowledge communicated by the tragedian player and puppeteer is even more inferior than that conveyed by the tragedian writer because it is an imitation of an imitation and therefore further removed from the truth.

Socrates felt that the tragic poetry that had preceded him did not support the moral or theoretical life, an endeavor that he believed was better served by philosophy. He suggested that imitation serves no healthy or true purpose. He even went so far as to suggest that it maimed decent men, except for a rare few. Poetic imitation does this by strengthening impulses that ought to be repressed. In experiencing ribald humor, buffoonery and the pleasures of the flesh and soul vicariously, people are transformed into the thing that is imitated. These things rule them and they became worse and more wretched as a result.

Socrates' criticisms are successful against ancient Greek theater, but how well do they hold up in relation to the use of theatrical forms by Christians today? Providentially, the Bible provides a basis for evaluating the validity of Socrates' arguments generally. Socrates is correct when he understood the makers of tragedy to be inventing the gods. God tells us that his ways are beyond human understanding (Isaiah 55:8, 9). The gap between God and man is unbridgeable by man. The only true knowledge that we can have of God is that which He chooses to reveal to us. God reveals Himself through His creation and His word but his clearest revelation is through His incarnate Son who embodies the word (John 1:14).

Therefore, the Bible and the Savior it reveals constitute the only mirror that gives us an accurate picture of our place in the universe, our responsibilities to God and the manner of discharging these responsibilities. The archaic Greeks, reliant as they were on the mythic imagination to mirror the cosmos, distorted even the testimony of the natural world to the existence of a great Creative intelligence. They created a world of gods in their own image. The Greek philosophers managed to discern the existence of an unknown god, but they were no more effective than the mythic poets in finding the truth about this Deity (Acts 17:23). Neither the mythic imagination nor the logic of the philosophers was adequate to discern and represent the truth. Socrates may have triumphed over the poets but it was a pyrrhic victory.

Yet, for all this, there is a place for reason in the detection of truth. In full acceptance of divine revelation and under the influence of the Holy Spirit, mankind is able to use sanctified reason to discern truth (Isaiah 1:18). To put it in philosophical terms, reason is necessary to the discovery of truth but not sufficient operating alone. If correct assumptions are accepted, reason can provide useful intellectual outcomes. Thus, taking as our starting point the supremacy of God's revelation of Himself and the nature of reality through His word and the life of His incarnate Son, theatrical imitation, whether based upon the mythic imagination, reason alone or the revelation of Scripture, is a less perfect method of representing or conveying truth than that contained in the word of God. Socrates is correct about imitation.

We can understand now why Jesus used no theatrical devices to gain attention and why He constantly focused on the Scriptures. We can also understand why it pleased God to save both Jews and Greeks through the foolishness of preaching (1 Corinthians 1:21). If ever the cultural relevance argument was compelling in relation to theater, it was compelling in relation to the Athenian Greeks of apostolic times. Yet, Paul engaged them at an entirely different level (Acts 17). The word of God, not religious drama or comedy, is quick and powerful and sharper than a two-edged sword in piercing to the depths of the heart (Hebrews 4:12). The word of God remains the truest mirror of the cosmos.

To draw attention to this word, Jesus and the apostles engaged in acts of kindness and healing. They drew the minds of their hearers to God's word through arresting preaching and the logic of their teaching. It was in contemplation of the word of God and the life of Christ that people were transformed: "But we all, with open face beholding as in a glass the glory of the Lord, are changed into the same image from glory to glory, even as by the spirit of the Lord" (2 Corinthians 3:18). The transforming power of the gospel is made effective through the contemplative and prayerful study of the word of God (1 Peter 1:23). God wants those who choose Him to be conformed to the image of His Son (Romans 8:29). Here is the secret to powerful witness. As Christ's life is formed within, the Christian becomes the light of the world (John 8:12). People will know that the Bible is true when they can see a living representation of God's word.

Thus, God's agencies for the conversion of the world's people are His living word in the Bible and His word living in His people. The example of one godly life will do more to attract people to the gospel than all the dramatic and comic troupes in Christianity today. It is because the Bible is not preached and lived as it ought to be that the power has largely disappeared from Christian witness and evangelism. As the Scriptures have lost their hold in the West, the vacuum has been filled by a resurgent paganism. The way back for Christian youth ministry is not to become more like paganism, either old or new, but by setting itself in clearer contrast with it in all of its forms.

Notes

[1] The following electronic sources have been useful in establishing the factual basis upon which my ideas in this chapter have been developed. **Britannica DVD 2000:** The origins of Western theatre; dithyramb; Satyrs and Silenus; Dance in classical Greece; Satyr play; Old Comedy; Theatre: the Middle Ages in Europe; Comedy, satire, and romance; Clown; Sacred Clown; & Mime and Pantomime. **Encarta 1993:** Drama and Dramatic Arts; Mask; & Puppets and Marionettes.

[2] I am indebted to my friend Kel Naughton, for this observation.

Chapter 3

MARKING THE MUSIC

The Rejection of Reason

The decade of the 1980s was a time of great intellectual ferment. The modernist or Enlightenment belief that there are universal standards and criteria of rationality was under threat within a number of academic disciplines. One academic rationalist who strenuously resisted the break from a universal rationality was Allan Bloom of the University of Chicago. In his 1988 book, *The Closing of the American Mind*, Bloom lamented, "Western rationalism has culminated in a rejection of reason" (240). But Bloom's efforts were not sufficient to prevent the disintegration of modernism. The displacement of reason as the ultimate arbiter of knowledge and values was simply too advanced to be reversed. When the Soviet satellite states in Eastern Europe began to collapse in 1989, the Enlightenment values that had ruled the world for two hundred years finally relinquished their cultural dominance in favor of pluralistic postmodernism.

While modernism retains many adherents, the West is now characterized by a multiplicity of social and cultural universes, each with its own irreducible rules of thinking and modes of engagement. Culturally, the emphasis is no longer on commitment to the rigorous use of reason but to the free expression of emotions and feelings. Absolutes, whether derived from revelation or reason, are rejected in favor of feel-good ideas and practices. Standards of evaluation are internal rather than external. Doing your own thing is the guiding principle of action. The social consensus that resulted in Western history from an adherence to religious tradition, Biblical revelation or reason, is now a thing of the past.

While the shift from the rational to the romantic or mythic imagination, as seen in the shift from modernism to postmodernism, is one of those periodic intellectual shifts that occur throughout Western history, Allan Bloom perceived in this change some very sinister consequences for education and society. In the rejection of reason in the universities, Bloom saw the seeds of future tyranny in the United States (240). There are good reasons for Christians to believe that Bloom is correct in his assessment of the dangers of tyranny resulting from the resurgence of irrationalism and the rise of philosophical nihilism.

These reasons are based not only on the degree of common ground that Christians can share with Bloom in his assessment of the philosophies that undergird postmodernism but also on the publicly verifiable certainties of Biblical prophecy. This theme will be taken up later in this chapter. At this point, however, it is necessary only to note that there are good reasons to take serious account of Bloom's warnings about the crisis of reason in higher education and the resulting potential for tyranny.

Whatever the ultimate merits of Bloom's analysis, it is clear that he was a shrewd observer of the changing tastes of his students and the practices that were impoverishing their souls and closing their minds. One of the student addictions that Bloom identified as a symptom of emerging irrationalism is rock music. His essay on the effects of rock music on education and youth generally is a compelling critique of what is now an almost universal passion among the young (68-81).

Something that Bloom wrote in this essay makes it highly relevant to an evaluation of the use of rock music and associated musical forms in Christianity today. Bloom treated the passion for rock music among the young as something alien to the church. He was evidently not aware of the emerging Contemporary Christian Music (CCM) movement or had no knowledge of the intrusion of this form of music into the churches. His trenchant criticisms of rock music therefore deserve the most serious attention by all Christians. Bloom's essay also has the advantage of providing a touchstone for relating rock music to the themes that have been explored earlier in this book. For these reasons, Bloom's criticisms provide a convenient vehicle for examining the impact of rock music upon young people and assessing its appropriateness for worship, ministry or evangelism.

It is important to a proper assessment of Bloom's criticisms of rock music to understand his reasons for making them. Bloom does not deal with rock music at the level of personal like or dislike or of supposed intergenerational differences. He describes how he instinctively sided with his students who responded to the newly emerging rock beat. He felt that they had real, if coarse, feelings rather than artificial or dead ones. That was before the full dimensions of the rock revolution had become obvious to him. Bloom's essay is primarily concerned with the effects of rock music upon liberal education. He is moralizing only to the extent that he expresses concern that rock music hinders the development of moral judgment in his students. Bloom wants his students to experience lives that are enriched by the liberal virtues of reason, tolerance and happiness.

While Bloom did not believe that the Bible was the only means to furnish a mind, he did believe that, without a book of similar gravity, read with the gravity of the potential believer, the mind would remain unfurnished. He believed that the 'great tradition,' by which he meant the great thinkers of history, had something profound to say to students. Bloom believed that rock music encourages passions and provides students with models that cannot possibly be implemented in their lives and which are inconsistent with those provided by liberal studies.

His concern was that a student who was actively engaged with rock music could not understand what the great tradition had to say to him or her and that prolonged engagement with rock music produced a person incapable of understanding its significance, even when the exclusive passion for rock music had passed. Bloom felt that an addiction to rock music, like a serious fling with drugs, sapped the energy of students and ruined their imaginations. He viewed rock music as junk food for the soul.

Little wonder, then, that Bloom felt that there was nothing in common between the world of the church and the world of adolescent addiction to rock music. If what he has to say about the inhibiting effect of rock music on the development of rational thinking, humane imagination and refinement of taste among his student is correct, there are enormous implications for the use of rock music in Christianity, especially with regard to youth ministry. It is therefore important to understand how Bloom arrived at his conclusions and to test their validity. If Bloom's conclusions are valid for liberal education, they will also be valid for Christian education and character formation.

Bloom notes that in the past, students were indignant at the censorship in the famous passages dealing with musical education in Plato's *Republic*, for they had experienced music as entertainment rather than as a matter of importance to political and moral life. His students now understand why Plato's Socrates took music so seriously in these dialogues. Their addiction to rock music confirms the importance that Socrates attaches to music in the preparation of rulers and citizens for a desirable republic. They are indignant because the censorship in the *Republic* seems to want to deprive them of their most intimate pleasure.

Plato's position regarding music, expressed simply by Bloom, is that rhythm and melody, accompanied by dance, are the barbarous expression of the soul. Bloom notes that Friedrich Nietzsche, who agrees substantially with Plato's analysis, saw music as the soul's primitive and primary speech, that is hostile to reason and that always dominates articulate speech that is added to it. In other words, according to Nietzsche, music will always exert a more powerful and immediate influence than the words or lyrics that are added to it. If such is the case, the notion that rock music can be sanitized by the addition of Christian lyrics is in serious difficulty. That is a critical issue in the evaluation of CCM to which we shall return later in this section.

As Bloom points out, Plato's position on the importance of music in education underscores his teaching that in order to take the spiritual temperature of an individual or society, one need only "mark the music" of that individual or society. For Plato, music provides a guide to the states of the souls of those living in a particular society. If such is the case, the implications for Christianity are immediately obvious. The type of music indulged by Christians may therefore be a useful indicator of spiritual temperature. Again, this is an important issue to which we will return shortly.

Bloom now situates the significance of rock music in the reaction against Enlightenment rationalism initiated by Jean Jacques Rousseau and Friedrich Nietzsche. He notes that Nietzsche in particular wanted to replenish the irrational sources of vitality in the West by encouraging Dionysian impulses and the music derived from it. Bloom then suggests that the single appeal of rock music is a barbaric appeal to undeveloped and untutored sexual desire. He adds that young people know that rock has the beat of sexual intercourse. That helps to explain Bloom's association of rock music with antinomianism, free sexual expression, anarchism, and mining of the irrational unconscious. By providing intense and premature ecstasy, rock music jades the soul, diminishes expectations and reduces enthusiasm for life.

Are Bloom's conclusions about the nature of rock music in the mid 1980s correct and, if so, do they hold today? There can be little doubt that Bloom was correct when he identified rock music as the most intimate pleasure of students of the mid 1980s. During the early 1980s, I was an external graduate student at the University of New England, Armidale, Australia. On my visits to the University, I stayed in various residential colleges of the University. On many occasions, it was almost impossible to work or sleep in my room because of the noise of blaring rock music. During my last residential visit to the University, I was so tired from lack of sleep after a few days that I was forced to leave the college to find alternative accommodation. Late one night, before I left the college, I was unable to sleep because of the noise, so I wandered through the college corridors. Rock music seemed to be pulsing from every room.

The day I decided to move out of the college, I went to the library to work but could still hear a driving beat. There was no rock playing in the library or its immediate environment but the persistent sound in my head was indistinguishable from the real thing. I knew then that it was time to move out of my room. On that last campus visit, the impact of the seemingly ubiquitous rock music on my performance was dramatic. I managed to complete less than half the work that I had planned. My subsequent experience of rock music on university campuses suggests that rock remains the most immediate and familiar of student gratifications.

Then, as now, rock music is the enemy of reason and reflection. There are no fine nuances with rock. One of its defining characteristics is its loudness. Without a driving beat and extreme loudness, rock loses its appeal. I cannot recall ever observing anyone voluntarily turn rock music down to listen to it. It seems that rock is a visceral rather than an aural experience. Satisfaction levels with rock seem to increase with increasing volume. The trancelike behavior at rock concerts also seems to correlate with the driving beat and the extreme loudness. Rock overwhelms the rational faculties. That explains why rock breaks down the barriers to free sexual expression and drug taking. It may also explain why the rock obsession seems to engender a lack of consideration for the rights of others.

Bloom is correct when he noted that the rock music of the mid

1980s was profoundly hostile to reason. He identifies Mick Jagger as the rock personality who, during the 1970s and early 1980s, epitomized best the orgiastic nature of rock music and its inherent nihilism. In explaining Jagger's influence, Bloom evokes the appeal of the possession dances and music of ancient Dionysian rites. He describes Jagger's musical persona until the age of forty as "the possessed lower-class demon and teen-aged satyr." Bloom also notes Jagger's role in legitimating drugs among the young.

There is no evidence that this situation has changed in the years since Bloom wrote. In fact, if anything, rock has become even more bizarre. Its continuing powerful influence upon the directions of youth culture indicates that the pendulum of Western history and culture has swung to the very extreme of Romantic irrationalism. Pop culture today reflects the pluralism and anti-rationalism of postmodernism (Grenz 1996, 37). Those who listen to rock music no longer believe that their world has a center or that reason can perceive a logical structure to the external universe. Rock music, with its appeal to pluralism, moral permissiveness and rebellion against authority, is characteristic of postmodernism (Veith, Jr. 1993, 105).

The truly frightening thing about the excesses and weirdness of rock culture today is that the first great experiment with moral permissiveness and postmodernism in the twentieth century paved the way for the tyranny of National Socialism. Germany, in the 1920s and 1930s, experienced the loss of a moral center that was unprecedented in the modern West. Both the rise of permissiveness and National Socialism were related to the decline in Christian morality that followed the popularization of Charles Darwin's theory of evolution in Germany.

The great popularizer of Darwin, Ernst Haeckel, played a significant role in the development of the "scientific racism" of National Socialism (Gasman 1971). The other significant figure in the eventual rise of National Socialism was Friedrich Nietzsche, who took Darwin's ideas to their logical conclusions, spurned Christian morality and promoted the revival of the Dionysian impulse in music. Ironically, it was the rise of Biblical criticism in Germany that paved the way for the enthusiastic acceptance of Darwin, Haeckel and Nietzsche.

Veith, Jr. (1994, 79) notes that the irrationalism and anti-human values of the postmodernists have already been tried once, with catastrophic results. He is referring to the rise of fascism in the early to mid twentieth century in Italy and Germany. Veith believes that, with the failure of communism, fascism is making a comeback. He warns that postmodernist theorists are reintroducing the ideas that gave us the Second World War and the Holocaust. Thus Veith arrives at a similar conclusion to Bloom—the rise of postmodernism may lead to tyranny. Significantly, both Veith and Bloom identify rock music as being essentially postmodernist.

Consequently, it is possible to read the state of our societies and the states of the souls of our youth in the ongoing obsession with rock music and its associated forms. For the majority of young people, rock continues to be, in Bloom's words, "a common culture of reciprocal communication and psychological shorthand." Rock is, as Bloom said, "as unquestioned and unproblematic as the air the students breathe." That is also largely true of society itself. Rock is the modern demonstration of the "power of music in the soul." Rock is the unconscious made conscious. Rock is what we brought back from our voyage to the underworld.

It is indeed strange that a form of music that possesses the minds and bodies of young people, and that is inextricably associated with drugs, permissiveness, and nihilism, should achieve such widespread acceptance in technologically advanced societies. It is even more bizarre that many schools should encourage this passion among their students by organizing dances and providing opportunities for students to form rock bands and participate in interschool competitions. Every effort is made to exclude alcohol and drugs from these activities but students know that this is an artificial distinction. Some schools have even included rock music as a subject offering. With high rates of youth suicide in many Western countries, this encouragement of mass possession among the young is a chilling indicator of the moral blindness that has taken root in the West.

Bloom's concerns about the decline of liberal education are well founded. The loss of the cultural consensus about the importance of liberal education, that has accompanied the rise of the postmodernist sensibility, has weakened and fragmented the influence of liberal studies. In many Western universities, the humanities are struggling to retain students and to avoid funding cuts. There are other reasons for this state of affairs, including the rapid reshaping of the West by technological advances and economic rationalism, but there can be little doubt that the cultural dominance of rock has contributed to the declining interest in liberal studies and the role models they offer.

The capacity of rock music to shape the cultural and moral landscapes of young people and their educational tastes makes it one of the most powerful formative influences operating in the West today. Rock has also been the major force in the creation of the emerging global youth culture, which has become the touchstone for all kinds of bizarre expressions of the irrational unconscious, from body piercing to extreme sports. History is replete with examples of popular enthusiasms that have touched most societies at some time. However, it is difficult to find an example of a global enthusiasm in the modern era that surpasses the passion for rock music among the young. Even soccer, the sport that arouses more enthusiasm worldwide than any other, does not have the same global reach as rock.

Rock is not only creating a world youth culture, it is also creating a world music based upon its rhythms. This may help explain why rock is becoming an integral part of the movements for world peace, the environment and the New Age. The exploration of the irrational unconscious in rock music not only breaks down the barriers to the spirituality of animist and spiritist cultures, including those reviving in the West, but also merges with the musical heritage of these cultures. Rock is therefore an important channel for the pre-Christian era to flow back into Western civilization.

It is not a coincidence that rock music is inseparable from dance in the West. The rhythmic beat of rock is made to order for uninhibited dancing. Rave dancing, where young people take the drug Ecstasy to enable them to increase their endurance for dance, is an emerging phenomenon that has associations with the possession dances of many cultures throughout the world. The attraction to body decoration and piercing in these cultures is evident among rave dancers. The direct experience of altered states of consciousness that is common to shamanistic dancing is rapidly becoming the common language of the emerging global village.

How do we explain the phenomenon of rock music, especially in the West? There are several compelling reasons why the answer to this question must be found in the spiritual realm. First, rock has risen to its position of cultural dominance in an era of declining commitment to Christianity in the West. Second, rock has not simply occupied the space vacated by Christianity in the lives of young people; it has been profoundly antagonistic to it. Third, this antagonism to the teachings of Christianity has not extended to all religions. Rock, as we have seen, is actually quite compatible with many religions and cultures. In this context, it is not difficult to see that rock's popularity must be explained in terms of the modern crisis of Christianity in the West.

Significantly, the crisis in Christianity not only explains the rise of rock music in the West but it also helps to explain the adoption of rock music within Christianity. The loss of Christian vitality in the West was due, in part, to the rise of the scientific worldview and a loss of confidence in the Bible. As confidence in the Bible waned, a spiritual and cultural vacuum was created among young people in the West that was largely filled by rock music. The loss of confidence in the Bible and the consequent decline in the Christian values that underpinned the West also served to remove any firm Christian benchmarks for evaluating the emerging rock phenomenon. Thus, for many Christians, their initial rejection of rock music transformed into grudging acceptance and then finally into enthusiastic commitment.

Whatever the reasons for it, the acceptance of rock within Christianity is astonishing. A form of music that overwhelms the senses and the capacity for reason and reflection is hardly the sort of thing that one would expect to find used as the vehicle for Christian evangelism and worship. Under such circumstances, it must be difficult to determine whether young people who are evangelized by such methods are attracted to Christianity or to the rock version of it. What sort of meaningful attachment to Christianity can take place under conditions in which rational thought is essentially impossible? How enduring will the commitment to Christ prove if rock is removed from the church life of young people evangelized in this way?

In commenting on the impact of rock music on the inner life of his students, Bloom notes how astounding it is that the best energies of society's best young people should be devoted to forming associations based upon "illusions of shared feelings, bodily contact and grunted formulas." He is astonished that such an indigestible phenomenon should become hardly noticed and routine. "It may well be," he comments, "that a society's greatest madness seems normal to itself." That conclusion could apply equally to much of Christianity today in relation to the acceptance of rock music and its variants in worship and evangelism.

This situation did not develop overnight, either in secular society or in the churches. But it has taken place in accordance with well-established principles of social or organizational change. Something that is as confronting to Western social values and Christian sensibility as rock music must be accepted or firmly rejected. There is no middle ground. If rock music is not firmly rejected, it eventually spreads to become a part of everyday experience that must be rejected constantly. Often the effort to maintain rejection becomes too difficult and grudging acceptance finally takes place. The intellectual dissonance or conflict that is created by this acceptance must be resolved, so the mind searches for reasons to support the change in attitude. Thus rock loses its outsider status and eventually becomes the new orthodoxy.

Hence the paralogical reasoning that is advanced in defense of rock music by many Christians today. Paralogy is illogical reasoning, especially of which the reasoner is unconscious. The intrusion of paralogical reasoning into Christianity explains why something that was perceived initially by Christians as strange and bizarre could become normal and acceptable to them. It also explains why those Christians who, by virtue of their education, should have little trouble detecting the deficiencies in the arguments for rock music seem strangely blind to these deficiencies. The extent of the intellectual crisis rock music is causing in youth ministry today can be determined by the company paralogy keeps. Paralogy is a defining characteristic of postmodernism.

A classic example of paralogy is the argument being advanced today by many Christians that the message of rock music is in the lyrics and not in the music. The assumption is that rock music is morally neutral and that it is the lyrics that determine whether rock is good or bad (Bacchiocchi 2000, 345). Thus, Christians who object to rock music in their churches are perceived or claimed to be ignorant or prejudiced or asserting nothing more than personal musical taste. These claims against those who reject "Christian rock" do not merit serious attention and can be cleared away readily. The *ad hominem*[1] arguments in relation to ignorance and prejudice constitute fallacies of relevance. The claim in relation to personal musical preference fails to account for those who like rock music but who reject it on grounds other than personal preference.[2] When such claims are advanced, it usually indicates that the position adopted by the one making the claims will not bear close scrutiny. So it proves, as the following discussion reveals.

If the lyrics of rock music carry its message and hence determine exclusively whether rock music is good or bad, then we should expect to find that the attraction to rock music has always been solely related to the lyrics. In other words, those who have been attracted to rock music have done so on the basis of its lyrics alone. So when the early forms of rock music became popular, it was only because the lyrics found an answering chord in people. Based on this argument, rock music was clearly bad because its lyrics focused on illicit sexual desire and rebellion against accepted religious, moral and social mores. It was bad because it encouraged young people to adopt permissive lifestyles. Thus, the badness of rock music resided in its lyrics and not to any extent in the music itself. How defensible is this position?

Sexually suggestive lyrics were not unknown in the era of popular music that preceded the emergence of rock music. Subversive and protest music also had a long tradition before the arrival of rock music. Yet, no form of music has ever been received with more enthusiasm than rock music or achieved such widespread dominance. To what can we attribute this development? While it is possible to explain some of the popularity of early rock music on the basis of the sexual suggestiveness of the lyrics, the evidence suggests that the attraction of rock music resided in the unique way in which the music matched and enhanced the lyrics. The rhythm and accentuated beat of rock music encouraged the same lack of inhibition in the physical domain as the lyrics did in the moral domain. It was a combination perfectly adapted to uninhibited dance and thus uniquely suited to young people. Add some popular performers and creative marketing and you have the most successful, commercial cultural package in history.

That outcome is not attributable to lyrics alone. If the lyrics of rock songs were the attraction today, we would be faced with the difficult task of explaining why so many otherwise conventional people want to immerse themselves constantly in banality, perversion or evil. This difficulty is made even greater by the fact that it is often hard to hear or comprehend rock lyrics because of unnatural vocal contortions or the sheer volume of the music. If we finally concede that the music is a major part of the attraction to rock, we are forced to admit that the music itself has helped cause the moral decline that has been linked with rock music since its emergence in the 1950s. It is not a coincidence that rock music is associated from its very beginning with hostility to Christian principles. Anything that influences people to cast off the requirements of God, whether alone or in concert with something else is inherently bad. The music of rock is therefore unavoidably a moral issue.

The validity of this line of thinking is seen in the way in which rock music functions within Christianity. If the message is carried within the lyrics alone, and the music is neutral, why adopt rock music at all? There are better lyrics available than those generally found in "Christian rock." The reason why rock music has been adopted in much of Christianity is that the taste for the music of rock, which has been developed in the secular world, has been imported into the churches. The addition of lyrics compatible with Christianity is simply the pretext for its widespread use in worship and evangelism. The passion for rock music, within and without Christianity, is for the music. That much is evident from the way in which reviews of "Christian rock" deal so minutely with the characteristics of the music. But the music of rock is not compatible with Christianity. It remains the language of those who have no regard for God. "Christian rock" is simply a way of forgetting God that passes for a way of remembering Him. The serious consequences of this trend are the focus of the following section.

The Return of Myth

When reason lost its cultural dominance in the late 1980s, the Western world was faced with two options. It could return to dependence upon God's revelation in the Bible or it could more fully embrace the pre-Christian myths of its past. Those myths were embodied in the Romantic imagination that had been vying with reason since the middle of the eighteenth century. Unfortunately, Darwinism and Biblical criticism had stripped away confidence in the Bible, so the slide into myth, which was evident in the late modern period, continued unchecked. Virtually no part of the modern West has been left untouched by the return of myth. Even science, the last remaining stronghold of modernism, is experiencing a revival of myth and mysticism.

Rock music is one of the main channels by which mythology has been able to flow back into Western civilization. Rock fulfils this role in two ways. First, it mocks the conventions of the West, thus loosening attachment to the ideals that undergird the Western experience. Mostly, these ideals have Christian origins. Second, rock is a perfect medium for expressing pagan mythologies, images and symbols. As we have noted, the resurgence of body piercing and decoration in the West is closely related to the rock culture and the weird, bizarre tastes that it encourages. Again, it is not coincidental that modern Western tribalism has emerged on the back of rock culture. In short, rock is the antithesis of everything that Biblical Christianity represents.

In Christianity, rock performs all the roles that Dionysian music played in the religion of ancient Greece. It induces an altered state of consciousness similar to the trance possession of the satyrs and encourages religious dancing. In reducing inhibitions, rock encourages the primacy of the emotions in religious experience. This is more in tune with the direct experience of Eastern religion than it is with the injunctions of Biblical religion. For example, God invites us to apprehend salvation through reason (Isaiah 1:18). He uses His word to reach the hearts of people. Jesus spent much of His time teaching. Paul promoted the primacy of the things that instruct and edify. He warned against confusion and disorder in worship (1 Corinthians 14:33, 40). In short, anything that breaks down appropriate inhibitions should be avoided in Christian worship and evangelism.

Increasingly, rock is the music of choice for youth worship and evangelism in the churches, providing a point of harmony between Christians of different persuasions. It breaks down the barriers between Christian denominations by encouraging an emphasis on praise and a corresponding disregard of doctrine. It is therefore perfectly adapted to the aspirations of ecumenism. It also has the added benefit of linking ecumenism with the emerging global culture. But shared illusions are still illusions and pretending otherwise will only cause Protestants to misapprehend the significant warning signs which suggest that these developments are helping to shape the global tyranny described in Revelation 13. Let me explain.

Jencks (1996, 6) uses a parable to describe the shift from modernism to postmodernism. He suggests that the temper of modernism is the New Protestant Reformation, in that it is Puritanical and exclusivist. On the other hand, he likens Post-Modernism to the New Counter-Reformation because of its emphasis on worldliness, lushness, variety and a spirituality that has a cosmic orientation based upon contemporary science. What Jencks is saying, in effect, is that the future will be profoundly antagonistic to Protestant spirituality. Jencks believes that the emerging global culture will be based upon the post-modern science of complexity, including recent cosmology, in which the universe is seen as a single, creative, unfolding event in which the evolution of life, mind and culture is perfectly natural and probably inevitable. Hence, it is no surprise when Jencks expresses his belief in the self-organization of matter or, as he labels it, "focussed evolution."

Jencks considers "focussed evolution" to be a deeply spiritual narrative (72). He believes that the universe is the measure of all things and that the story of the universe, in its attempt to reach yet higher levels of organization, is able to orient a global civilization (77). Significantly, Jencks believes that the story of an unfolding universe will form the organizing principle for historical religions, as well as science and other cultural discourses (7). Such a vision of the future is not compatible with any Biblical view of the origins of the universe or the future of humanity. It does, however, represent a view that is fundamentally compatible with the notion of theistic evolution introduced to the Roman Catholic Church by French Jesuit, Pierre Teilhard de Chardin. Chardin's conception of an intelligent guiding principle in evolution, rather than chance or, in Jencks' case, the principle of self-organization of matter, is just as much a repudiation of the Biblical account of our origins and our future as the view that the universe is engaged in an evolutionary unfolding. Significantly, the ideas of purposeful evolution or evolutionary unfolding of the universe are found in the New Age movement.

What we are seeing is the rapid dissolution of the boundaries between evolutionary science, New Age spirituality and Teilhardian theistic evolution. Each of these belief systems is compatible with the emerging global spirituality. Each of these belief systems is incompatible with a Biblical understanding of the origins, purpose and future of humanity. The new global spirituality can accommodate any species of thought as long as it is not derived from an acceptance of Biblical authority in all matters of belief and practice. Jencks aptly speaks of postmodernism as the New Counter-Reformation for it rejects the foundational commitment to the Bible as the infallible word of God.

Where this emerging global spirituality or consciousness is leading us can be seen in the pantheistic view of God that is intrinsic to it. Pantheism is the belief that God is everything and everything is God. It is the one conception of God that is capable of uniting the disparate elements of world religions. It thrives in the interfaith movement, which has a great deal of common ground with the New Age movement (Pollitt 1996, 149). Teilhard de Chardin was profoundly attracted to pantheism. Significantly, rock music and pantheism have common African roots (Bacchiocchi 2000, 62). Pantheism, with its belief in a God within individuals and the natural world, is reflected in the features of the possession-trance type of music that is found in West Africa. It is also significant that the humanistic/pantheistic view of God as a natural process is pervasive in our secular society. Pantheism therefore provides an important link between religion and contemporary science. Like pantheism, rock bridges religious and cultural divisions.

Rock is therefore the one form of music capable of expressing global spirituality. It is hostile to Biblical religion and destroys the Christian claim to exclusive revelation. Rock is opening the door to the return of myth in the churches. The widespread use of rock in Protestantism today is seriously compromising Biblical authority and the integrity of worship and evangelism. The German philosopher, Arthur Schopenhauer, in attempting to explain why music was the most powerful and penetrating of the arts, suggested that music was a copy of the will itself.[3] He saw music as an analogue of the emotional life. If Schopenhauer is correct, as I believe him to be on this matter, then it is also true that our will goes with the music that we choose. The widespread adoption of rock music in the churches is therefore a startling portent of the imminent death of Protestantism.

The general death of the Protestant sensibility is necessary to the triumph of a global spirituality, for Protestantism, with its recognition of the authority of the Bible, is the one thing that cannot be harmonized with it. The demise of Protestantism is therefore the one essential precondition to the development of a truly global society. As we are seeing in the fracturing of nation states, economic or technological globalization is not sufficient to create a world society. A world spirituality that is acceptable to all the major religious traditions and secularists is needed to accomplish this end. When it is accomplished, the Bible tells us that a global religious tyranny will follow (Revelation 13:15-17). The tyranny will be established by false miracles and enforced through economic means. All who live on the earth will be required to worship the image of the beast. This means compliance with religious requirements that conflict with those enjoined by God. Thus, Christians will be forced to choose between loyalty to God's commandments and death. Those Christians who choose to compromise their loyalty to God at this time may save their lives in the short term but will lose eternal life.

The first beast in Revelation 13 is clearly a religio-political power because it accepts worship or spiritual submission and inspires fear and wonder throughout the world. It receives its power from the dragon or Satan. It is a power that commits blasphemy (Verse 6). In Scripture, blasphemy is committed when a mere man claims to be God or to have the power to forgive sins (John 10:33; 2 Thessalonians 2:4; and Luke 5:21). The beast is identified with the number of a man (Revelation 13:18). The beast is therefore a man who poses as God and as one with the power to forgive sins. He sits at the head of a giant religious system for only a vast system could hope to exercise the influence that impresses and intimidates the whole world (Revelation 13:4). The only system that meets these criteria, as the reformers so clearly observed, is the papal system.

Yet, the beast receives aid not only from the dragon but also from the false prophet (Revelation 16:13). A prophet is one who speaks on God's behalf. A false prophet is one who claim to speak on behalf of God but who has a message that is not in accordance with God's word and who turns people away from God's commandments (Deuteronomy 13:1-5). In the Book of Revelation, it is a religious confederacy that plays a role in encouraging submission to the beast power or the papal system (Revelation 17:5). It is a religious confederacy that has become enamored with the papal system and has, through ecumenical alliance, given its power and strength to it (Revelation 17:13).

The power that unites the global confederacy is Spiritism (Revelation 16:13, 14). It is through the spirits of devils, and their power to work miracles, that this unholy alliance is able to bring under its influence the Spiritism of paganism and the spiritualism of apostate Christianity. Spiritualistic manifestations will be used to draw the unwary into the web of deception. God has warned of the methods to be used so that all might discern the nature of the error that will be pressed upon the Christian world. He has also given firm criteria for testing the credentials of those who advocate that spiritualistic manifestations can be used as a safe guide to understanding God's will (Isaiah 8:19, 20). These criteria tell us that those who do not uphold God's law and all of His revealed will as contained in the Bible are to be rejected as false guides. Only those who apply the Protestant principle of testing all things by the Bible will be safe from deception.

We are seeing today the development of a world economy and a world culture. Rapid advances in communications technology are driving economic interdependence and cultural integration. At the same time, regional conflicts and terrorism threaten to bring the world to the edge of chaos. The convergence of these factors provides the perfect pretext for imposing global spiritual requirements that are consistent with the beliefs of the warring factions. When circumstances demand it, the peoples of the world will be prepared to give up certain freedoms to secure what they believe will be a period of peace and prosperity for all. Many who previously upheld the principles of democracy will advocate the restriction of liberty in the name of the greater good. The loss of democratic rights will seem a small price to pay for world peace.

In the early 1990s, the triumph of democracy over Communism was seen to be the beginning of a new era of reduction in world tensions. But that hopeful scenario has not eventuated. If anything, the dangers are now greater than at the height of the Cold War. Democracy itself is no guarantee that despotism will not arise, as the histories of ancient Greece and the Weimar republic attest. If conditions become extreme enough, any democracy can be destabilized. At the same time as international political instability has reached a dangerous level, the Ecumenical and Inter-Faith movements are holding out a potential solution. This convergence of global political and religious trends is ominous in the light of Biblical prophecy.

In this context, Bloom's warning about the possibility of tyranny in the world's most powerful democracy deserves serious consideration by all who value their liberties. His description of the role of rock music in the decline of the cultural rationality of the United States should arouse Christians to a sense of their danger in adopting this form of music. Rock music degrades the faculties of reason and discernment. These are the very things that we need most in the confused spiritual environment of the early twenty-first century. Therefore, the issue of rock music in Christianity is not an issue of personal or group preference or sincerity but rather an issue of the survival of Biblical Christianity itself. The extent of the incursion of rock music in the churches is a measure of the extent to which the churches are embracing the modern revival of myth.

Notes

[1] Arguments directed to the characteristics of a person rather than to the issues under discussion.

[2] In fact, the claim is self-reflexive and poses a serious threat to the

position of the one making it. That is, it might equally apply to the one making the claim, especially where the person's arguments are shown to be inadequate, thus raising questions concerning the reasons why the person continues to hold to a position that has been disconfirmed by rational argument. Ironically, one such argument might be personal preference.

[3] Britannica DVD 2000, music: The concept of dynamism.

Chapter 4

DIVIDED HEARTS

Lovers of Pleasures

I have in my library a collection of moral stories for children and youth, put together in the early twentieth century, mostly from nineteenth century Protestant magazines and journals.[1] The collection contains a number of stories concerning the devastating effects of such practices as drinking alcohol, gambling, attending the theater, and dancing. Yet, the overwhelming majority of stories are concerned with the influence of seemingly small decisions and acts upon the development of character and life's outcomes. Today, many of the issues raised in these stories would be considered somewhat trivial and their treatment exaggerated. However, the intent of the writers is clear. They are concerned to give unambiguous guidance on issues of importance to success in the Christian life.

There can be little doubt that our Christian writers of a century or more ago, were they alive today, would be concerned to warn against the prevailing evils in society. They would have much to concern them. The constant broadcast or screening of rock music, violence, corruption, nudity, adultery, fornication, and blasphemy would be a major concern, as would be alternative lifestyles, drugs, body piercing and decoration, violent computer games and extreme sports. They would undoubtedly be alarmed to discover the extent of the Christian compromise with these evils. But what they would probably find truly astonishing, apart from the difficulties of getting their views published in their own denominational magazines and journals, is the extent to which many of the prevailing evils are used to promote the moral and spiritual development of young people.

What would our writers of centuries past make of the rock music reviews, movie reviews, and articles on sports heroes and extreme sports that feature prominently in youth magazines today? It is likely that they would feel that Paul's prophecy of the last days had been realized (2 Timothy 3:1-5). Paul speaks of a time when the distinction between the world and the church would be almost obliterated. Christians would have a form of godliness but would deny the power of the gospel by exhibiting the characteristics of the unrighteous. These professed Christians participate in the leisure practices of the unrighteous to the extent that they are described as lovers of pleasures more than lovers of God. This is parallel to Luke's warning that, when Jesus comes the second time, genuine Christian faith will be in short supply (Luke 18:8).

Paul specifically warns that disobedience to parents will be a greater than usual problem in the last days. This problem is manifested in the churches by a widespread rejection of religion by many young people who have been raised in Christian homes. Those youth and young adults who do stay in the churches often want to change their churches into their own image. They reject the religious forms and practices of their parents and despise the limitations that they feel are placed upon them. Thus, they become especially vulnerable to the deceptive teachings of those who have a form of godliness but who help bring perilous times upon God's people by agitating their corrupt viewpoints (2 Timothy 3:13). Paul's solution to this problem is to encourage Timothy, a young minister, to continue to believe and practice those things that he has learned as a child from the Holy Scriptures (2 Timothy 3:14, 15). It is to the Bible that young people must look if they are to successfully navigate the perilous times of the last days. Happily, many beautiful Christian young people continue to look to the Bible for inspiration and guidance.

Paul instructed Timothy to flee from youthful lusts (2 Timothy

2:22). Yet, the modern entertainment and leisure industries, with their huge resources and influence, saturate the world with images, sounds and experiences that encourage these very things. Young people need to be warned and instructed about the dangers that these industries pose to their morality and spirituality. Yet, when young people should be able to rely upon the guidance of older Christians in these matters, they often find themselves exposed to the erroneous idea that these industries have much to offer them in their personal and spiritual development. Thus, when many Christian people of influence should be standing as guardians of the interests of young people, they betray this sacred trust. While the full dimensions of this betrayal are not yet evident, some idea of its distressing magnitude can be gained by examining the Biblical principles that are relevant to questions of popular culture.

Cinema

Job made a figurative covenant between his conscience and his eyes that he would not allow his eyes to seduce his heart into impure thoughts (Job 31:1, 7). The issue was specifically related to gazing upon a young woman in a way that would suggest impure thoughts. David determined to set no wicked thing before his eyes and resolved that he would not allow the works of those who had turned aside from God to cling to him (Psalm 101:3). If David had held firmly to these principles throughout his life, he would not have permitted his eyes to linger on Bathsheba and thus open the door to a grievous sin. Jesus indicated that the impure appreciation of feminine beauty, occurring outside of the marriage relationship, is adultery (Matthew 5:27, 28). The outward act simply reflects the inner thoughts. Paul knew that we become what we habitually allow ourselves to view or consider (2 Corinthians 3:18). We are to think on those things that are pure and lovely and of good report (Philippians 4:8). John pointed out that the lust of the eyes is equivalent to love of the world and does not come from the Father

(1 John 2:16).

These principles suggest that we should avoid, as far as possible, those places or activities that suggest impure thoughts. It may not always be possible in a sinful world to avoid seeing some things that we would rather not see. Yet, we certainly can avoid the second look. Unless we do so, the heart will go with the eyes and the mind will soon consent to sin. Accordingly, those who choose to attend the cinema or to view television, video or DVD movies open their lives to a great evil. It is impossible to expose yourself to violence, nudity, immorality, corruption and almost all forms of deviance and retain purity of mind. Movie watching by professed Christians is a sure sign of a divided heart.

The movie reviews that can be found in Christian youth magazines and on Christian web sites display a lack of Biblical understanding and spiritual discernment that can only be explained in terms of alienation from God and a corresponding darkening of understanding (Ephesians 4:18). Christian apologists for movies are in the grip of a strong delusion. They are spiritually blind and, consequently, can no longer reason effectively. They call darkness light and light darkness (Isaiah 5:20).

If movies are safe for Christians to watch, then why is it necessary to have movie reviews written by Christians for other Christians? Should not the regular reviews be sufficient? If the answer is that we need Christian movie reviews because some movies may present material that is offensive to Christians, then we have a tacit acknowledgement that all movies are not necessarily appropriate for Christians to watch. But who is to decide that one movie is appropriate and not another? What seems innocent to one may be a cause of sin to another. There are Christian movie reviews on the Internet and viewer responses to these reviews that conflict sharply. One Christian thinks that a particular movie is offensive while another extols its virtues. The reviewer and the respondent are united only in their attachment to movies. Are Biblical principles so unclear that these matters simply become a matter of opinion? When clear Biblical tests are applied, they indicate that movies are not suitable recreation for Christians. If you reject these criteria, there is no value in any further appeal to the Bible—anything goes! One Christian supporter of movies on the Internet implicitly recognized this by indicating that Christians should simply ignore the offensive elements of a particular movie and focus on the positive elements. On this view, there is really no basis upon which offensive material could ever be judged to have reached a rejection threshold. If some offensive material is permissible, then all offensive material is permissible.

Some defend movies on the basis that the Bible contains many accounts of sin and evil. It is true that the Bible presents sin in its true light, but it never does so in an offensive way. Human sins and frailties are mentioned only to the extent necessary to give readers a sense of their need of salvation and to provide guidance on the issues of life. Unlike the movies, the Bible presents God's plan for eradicating sin and evil. The Bible never glorifies sin and never presents immorality or violence as a matter of entertainment or fun. Ironically, the movies create an imaginary world and impoverish real life, while the Bible records real life and enriches the imagination. Movies hold out the promise of a life that can never be, while the Bible offers a life of intense satisfaction now and an eternal future beyond the limits of earthly imagination (1 Corinthians 2:9).

A refusal to follow the path that God has revealed always results in a loss of spiritual discernment and the subsequent adoption of spiritual delusions (John 7:17). A spiritual delusion is one of the bleakest states of mind into which a Christian can lapse, for a delusion is by nature indiscernible to the person who is in its grip. People in a delusional state have no internal resources to guide them safely. Such a person remains captive to the mind of Satan unless God intervenes in some way and he or she is willing to submit to what God has revealed in His word.

The movie industry is committed to box office success. Movie themes are chosen on the basis of their appeal to human fantasies and illicit desires. Producers, directors and actors are united only in their aversion to Biblical principles, for it is these principles they fear most. Should these principles become established widely in society, the movie industry would go into severe decline. For this reason, every species of error is portrayed and glorified on the screen and Biblical Christianity denigrated at every opportunity. Movies have nothing to teach Christian young people and will only pervert the imagination. Whether or not the counsel is heeded, older Christians have an obligation to warn young people that movies provide Satan with direct access to their hearts and minds.

Extreme Sports

Our time and our physical powers are a gift from God and are to be preserved for His service. It is our duty to glorify God in our bodies (1 Corinthians 6:20). These Biblical principles reveal that it is wrong for Christians to needlessly expose themselves to the possibility of injury or death. Protection has been promised for those who have accepted the great commission to take the gospel to the world. Yet, Jesus revealed in His response to Satan's temptation to cast Himself off the pinnacle of the temple that it is wrong to improperly presume upon God's protection (Matthew 4:5, 6). Thus, to voluntarily risk injury or death in extreme sports, purely for the sake of exhibition, excitement or pleasure, is to sever one's connection with Christ and to venture upon Satan's ground. Extreme sports include such activities as paragliding, Motocross, snowboarding, downhill skiing, wakeboarding, skateboarding, abseiling, rock climbing, bungee jumping and white water rafting, although any high-risk physical activity is an extreme sport.

With such clear Biblical guidance available, it is astonishing to find extreme sports used widely in youth ministry today. The employment of such activities in youth ministry is usually justified on the basis that extreme sports develop the self-esteem and confidence of young people and lead to greater group cohesion. The justification sounds plausible but only because we have been conditioned by the New Age movement to believe that success in life is the result of releasing the forces that are hidden within us. The message that is repeated endlessly today by advocates of the human potential movement is that you can release your potential by confronting your fears and challenging your limits. The philosophy of extreme sports that emerges from the human potential movement is based upon the belief that terror is transformational. Extreme sports are therefore seen as a way of developing the spiritual and mental resources of young people. Living life to the maximum in an adrenaline-charged round of activities has become the norm for many Christian youth today.

It is true that God places a high value upon self-development. We have an obligation to develop our talents for service (Matthew 25:14-30). Yet, self-esteem is not self-development. Self-esteem results from looking inward and is an expression of the unregenerate human heart (Jeremiah 17:9). On the other hand, self-development is based upon an accurate evaluation of our lives against the external, infallible standard of the Bible and submission of our talents to God (2 Corinthians 13:5). The strength of self-esteem is human performance, while the strength of self-development is reliance upon God's grace in every circumstance. Every part of our existence is to be held open to God's sanctifying power (1 Thessalonians 5:23). Our bodies and health are to be preserved for service. Self-development is never accomplished through needless exposure to potential injury or death. Bringing youth to Christ and training them for service is greatly impeded by involvement in extreme sports.

One of my relatives, a youth pastor of extensive experience, related to me some years ago his assessment of the effects of various outdoor activities on the spiritual receptivity of young people. His experience was that exposure to highly exciting activities at youth camps, especially motorized activities of various types, made it almost impossible for camp staff to influence young people for Christ. This problem did not manifest itself to the same extent with less exciting outdoor activities.

The extent of the dangers that extreme sports pose to Christianity is evident among those who share the human potential movement's commitment to pushing the outer limits of physical risk or human endurance. It is no coincidence that the New Age movement, with its emphasis on developing human potential, embraces the spirituality of the North American Indians. The leadership development practices of the North American Indians often involved trials of strength or endurance, aided by strength received from the Great Spirit. Until the end of the nineteenth century, the Mandan Indians of North Dakota practiced a ceremony that was extremely physically and psychologically demanding (Maybury-Lewis 1992, 208). Young Mandans were hoisted and hung by skewers through the skin on their chests and backs. They were weighed down by buffalo skulls tied to their arms and legs and prodded with spears to add to their ordeal. They were tortured after they were let down. Those who were able to endure the four-day ceremony in stoic silence often went on to become tribal leaders. Such practices were supposed to develop inner strength. An uncomfortably similar ethic pervades the executive development programs of Japan and some leadership programs available in the West.

The ceremony practiced by the Mandan Indians was designed to put participants in touch with the Great Spirit who pervaded nature. By overcoming the physical and psychological ordeal in silence, participants became one with the Great Spirit and hence one with the natural world. Again, it is no coincidence that the rise of extreme sports has coincided with the rise of New Age spirituality and environmental consciousness. Extreme risk turns the focus inwards and helps participants to get in touch with themselves in a way that highlights the unity of the natural world. The taking of physical risks is therefore a way of experiencing the natural world through the enhancement of the senses. The philosophy of extreme sports therefore blends seamlessly with the world's mystical nature traditions.

Significantly, in the context of the Mandan experience, the revival of body jewelry in the West has reached the stage where some devotees suspend their bodies by the insertion of multiple hooks through their skin and flesh. This type of behavior may still shock us but it is no different in principle to involvement in extreme sports, in which the demand for adrenaline-charged experiences breaks down the barriers of self-restraint and spiritual discrimination. Extreme sports turn the mental and spiritual focus inward and open the door to New Age concepts. Take a group of young people who have shared such experiences and you have the conditions for an almost impenetrable group think.

Body Piercing and Decoration

Few aspects of Western culture have been untouched by the modern descent into myth. One of the more obvious changes in the West is the revival of body piercing and decoration. Both practices are forbidden in Scripture (Leviticus 19:28; Deuteronomy 14:1; Jeremiah 16:6). Humans are made in the image of God and to pierce or cut the flesh for ceremonial or decorative purposes, as in tattooing, body piercing, or scarification of the flesh, is to deface the image of God in humanity. That is evident in the self-mutilation that was characteristic of the prophets of Baal (1 Kings 18: 28). Body painting and decoration for ceremonial, social or decorative purposes also defaces the image of God in humanity and is likewise abhorrent to God. For example, Jezebel used visible cosmetics and painted her face (2 Kings 9:30; Jeremiah 4:30; Ezekiel 23:40). Specifically, the practice involved enlarging the eyes by highlighting them with a black mineral powder, in a manner that is similar to the use of mascara and eyeliner today.

Body piercing and body decoration are usually found together in tribal groups. These activities embody animist, spiritist and shamanistic beliefs and destroy the human dignity of those who practice them, whether in a tribal or a Western context. The emergence of ear, facial, tongue, navel, nipple and genital piercing and body suspension in the West is distressing for it indicates that many people are in bondage to evil spirits. In the Bible, self-mutilation is associated with spirit possession (Mark 5:1-20). The only hope of liberty from the defilement of body piercing is the presence of the Spirit of the Lord (2 Corinthians 3:17).

While the more extreme forms of body piercing are relatively rare among young people who have been raised as Christians, there are several practices in contemporary youth ministry or Christianity generally that break down the barriers to these practices. One such practice in youth ministry is face painting and decoration. Face painting is often associated with clowning or miming but may be used independently of these activities for such diverse reasons as performance art, group or team identification, and entertainment. Face painting, although seemingly innocuous, defaces God's image in young people and exposes them to the influence of evil spirits. What seems innocent at first may end in the spiritualistic bondage of body piercing.

Another practice that has diminished resistance to body piercing among young people who have been raised as Christians is the widespread use of visible cosmetics by Christian women. Despite the ancient association with rebellion, paganism or prostitution, cosmetics are respectable in most Christian circles today. The practice of using cosmetics by Christian women seemed innocent for decades until face painting and body decoration came into vogue among young people. Then, it was impossible for adult Christians who used or approved of cosmetics to argue consistently that there was anything sinister in the emerging practices of face painting or body decoration. Young people who wanted to engage in these practices could argue that, if cosmetics were acceptable, it was inconsistent to suggest that face painting or body decoration were unacceptable practices in Christianity.

A third practice that has opened the door to the more extreme forms of body piercing among young people of Christian background is ear piercing by Christian women. The piercing of the ear for earrings revived in the twentieth century.[2] The practice was widely adopted by many Christian women although it comes under the prohibition of the Bible. While body piercing was restricted to the ears, it seemed as innocuous as the use of cosmetics. Yet, when body piercing became more extreme, Christians who practiced or approved ear piercing were left without a coherent defense against it. Decades before Satan reintroduced extreme body piercing and decoration into Western society, he neutralized the potential opposition to these practices by seducing many Christians into accepting the less abhorrent versions of them. The result is that young people are not being educated to avoid these soul-destroying practices.

God's purpose is that His people be distinguished by their avoidance of the decorative arts in relation to dress and adornment (Hosea 2:13; 1 Timothy 2:9; 1 Peter 3:1-5). As we have seen, our bodies are the temple of the Holy Ghost and must only be used to glorify God. The use of jewelry to adorn the body temple misrepresents what God approves. Characteristics that God approves in His people are taught by the manner in which the ancient sanctuary was decorated. The gold in the ancient sanctuary was found on the inside, not the outside. God prefers the inner beauty of character to external beauty (1 Samuel 16:7).

The use of jewelry for adornment also destroys the distinctiveness that God desires His people to possess. It is important that a line of distinction be drawn between those who serve God and those who serve other gods. The piercing of the ears and the use of gold and silver earrings is known from antiquity and is associated with Eastern mysticism today. Women in Nepal hoard their gold in their ears. There is a supposed double benefit in that gold, being a yang or male quality, is thought to bring equilibrium to the life of the wearer of the earrings (Steed 1978, 10). The ear is also thought of as a microcosm of the body and remains important in acupuncture.

The wearing of jewelry is an act of self-exaltation. Humility and self-denial are much more appropriate for those whose sins have cost the infinite sacrifice of the Son of God. There is a charm and influence in simplicity that is unavailable to those who exalt themselves. Those who pierce their ears for the wearing of jewelry and who wear visible cosmetics are in the same kind of bondage to self as those who engage in body piercing and decoration. The respectable form of bondage may be less upsetting than the extreme form, but it is still bondage. Those who have the best interests of young people at heart will reject both forms and teach them to do likewise.

Dress

Our minds go with the way that we dress and the ways that we dress reflect our state of mind. Therefore, our dress communicates a significant amount about ourselves. The signals that we send through our dress are picked up accurately and we are often treated in a manner that is consistent with our dress. A lack of modesty by women invites illicit attentions. Women who dress like men enjoy less respect from them than those who dress in a distinctively feminine and modest way. Dress either invites confidence or it destroys it. Many of those who believe that the way we dress is a personal matter and irrelevant to the business of life give the lie to this belief when faced with a career or job interview. It is when they are trying to give the best impression possible that they strive to be less individual and more conforming to acceptable dress conventions.

Commonly, the best advice in relation to dressing for an important interview sounds remarkably similar to the dress principles of the Bible. Men are counseled to be understated in the way that they present themselves. Women are counseled against wearing revealing clothes, bright colors, gaudy makeup and excessive jewelry that distract attention from the way in which the interviewee meets the desirable personal qualities of the position. As first impressions are very powerful, and as we never get a second chance to make a good first impression, often the outcome of an interview is decided in the first few minutes.

Similarly, the way that we dress is important to our Christian witness and spiritual development. It is therefore an important part of youth ministry. Yet, too often, effective youth ministry is undermined by a lack of attention to Biblical principles of dress and adornment. Immodest or inappropriate dress by either sex can corrupt an otherwise excellent program by leading to an undesirable familiarity between the sexes. God designed that an appropriate distinction should be maintained in the way that men and women dress (Deuteronomy 22:5). Young women who dress like men become a stumbling block to young men. The moral tone of the program is lowered and the results are disappointing.

The corruption of dress standards in youth ministry is aided and abetted by the demoralizing effects of cinema, television, advertising, fashion, rock and sports and by the enthusiasm for such destructive practices as clowning, miming and drama. The resulting loss of discrimination as to what is appropriate dress for Christian young people adds further to the hurtful influence of the other unhelpful practices that are undermining the spiritual identity and well-being of young people. Any youth ministry program that fails to provide appropriate and timely counsel to young people on issues of dress and spirituality cannot hope to counteract the enormous social influences on young people to conform to dress practices and mores that degrade their dignity and weaken their attachment to Christ.

The widespread disregard of Biblical principles of dress by young people of Christian background is part of the wider problem of inappropriate dress by many older Christians. The power of example is important in changing the attitudes of young people. Many of these young people are dressing the way they do because they fear a lack of conformity to the dress standards of their peers. When they see the power of the gospel manifested in the way their parents and youth leaders dress, it is more likely that they will desire to live outside the powerful peer influences that shape their attitudes to dress matters.

Many young people, devoid of guidance on the issues of dress and adornment, now present themselves for worship dressed casually. They may reason that God is not concerned with how they dress but is more interested in their attendance. It is true that God desires their worship but it is not true that He is unconcerned with how they present at worship. In whatever we do we are to bring glory to God. If we present for worship dressed in a manner more befitting attendance at a rock concert, we do not bring glory to God. It is not our prerogative to decide the manner in which we will worship God.

Some object that God accepts diverse styles of dress and that the matter of dress is a cultural issue. God does take account of various cultural differences and accepts the worship of those who honor him by dressing modestly and appropriately within the acceptable bounds of cultural expression. Yet, the principle of acceptable cultural difference in dress is not an unbounded principle. There are limits to what is acceptable within each culture and it is a dishonor to God to ignore these limits in the name of cultural diversity.

Young people have been counseled to flee youthful lusts. To help them do this, God requires that young people submit themselves to the Godly counsel of their elders (1 Peter 5:5). Satan directs his rage against young people and there is a need for constant vigilance on their part that they do not accept principles of dress, amongst other things, that will give their adversary access to their lives (1 Peter 5:8). Satan is playing a deadly game with any young person who takes the matter of dress lightly. By dressing in accordance with the principles of simplicity, modesty and appropriateness on all occasions, young people can do much to protect themselves from unnecessary temptation.

Emotions

Life without emotion is dry and sterile. Yet, while emotions are wonderfully enriching when expressed within the bounds of God's law and reason, they are not a suitable foundation for the Christian life. God desires that our beliefs and actions be grounded in a mature understanding of His purposes (1 Corinthians 14:20). When God writes His law is in our minds and hearts, we delight to do His will. God wants us to appreciate His love with our minds (Isaiah 1:18). He wants us to worship Him in a way that enhances our understanding and extends our appreciation for Him. Christ is to be lifted up so that sinners might be drawn to Him.

The type of worship that meets these criteria is primarily cognitive (Ecclesiastes 5:1, 2). There should be an emphasis on the appreciation of God's word. It is God's word accepted into the life that has transforming power (1 Peter 1:23). While music and singing should express praise to God, words and music should be carefully chosen to reflect all the attributes of a Holy God. Care should be taken to ensure that songs are not overly repetitious or too narrowly focused. Hymns and songs that reflect sound doctrine and which are suitable for the occasion should be selected and music should play its important and enjoyable role in worship without becoming its central component. Particular care should be taken that special musical items do not crowd out the opportunity for the congregation to participate in singing.

The worship experience should bring honor and glory to God and uplift, encourage, instruct and edify the worshippers. True worship will draw worshippers out of themselves to love God and others more deeply. In worship that is acceptable to God, sensibilities will be aroused and worshippers will leave the house of God more distrustful of self, more confident in the goodness and mercy of God, and more determined to love and obey God with all their hearts.

In relation to youth ministry, these principles should apply in both worship and evangelism. It is particularly important that young people develop knowledge of God's word. It is through personal experience of God's word that young lives will be touched for Christ. Young people should be taught true principles of worship and conversion. It is important that young people understand that good feelings are not the aim of worship but its result. When God is honored and the worshippers edified, the sense of happiness and joy that results is God's gift to them.

Youth evangelism, worship and nurture no longer consistently reflect these foundational principles. The trend in youth ministry today is to focus activities around the central elements of youth culture rather than the word of God. The emphasis is shifting from the direct preaching or teaching of God's word to indirect forms of communication such as theater and music. There are a number of consequences of this shift. First, God's word is denied its full impact. Reading, study, meditation, preaching and teaching are God's appointed methods for the apprehension of His word. When we are transformed by God's word, our lives may witness to its transforming power, thus leading others to search it for themselves, but the witness of a Godly life is not meant to displace the forms of proclamation of His word that God enjoins. Some may argue that theatrical forms of communication arouse interest in God's word, but experience indicates that where such forms of communication are used at all, they invariably severely diminish or displace the preaching or teaching of God's word.

Second, while our emotions are involved in the acceptance of God's word, God desires that His word be understood and received with our minds. It is when we understand by the Holy Spirit what God has done for us in Christ and what He want to do in us that our emotions are properly aroused. To arouse the emotions without first arousing the mind to action is to shift the locus of control in spiritual matters from the cognitive or rational to the affective or emotional domain. The resulting emotional form of religion that is encouraged by this shift has often brought the gospel into disrepute by the excesses that it encourages. Therefore, large-scale worship and evangelistic events that encourage a highly charged emotional climate through theatrical devices, while de-emphasizing the proclamation of the gospel through preaching and teaching, are not safe places for youth.

Third, the shifting emphasis from direct to indirect modes of communication of the gospel changes the focus of youth ministry in radical ways. Instead of beholding Jesus as presented in Scripture, with an emphasis on all aspects of His character, worshippers are encouraged to focus on their own perceived needs to feel good and to have self-esteem. It means that worship functions less as contemplation of God and His characteristics, which draws us out of ourselves, and more on the factor of personal satisfaction from the worship experience, which draws us into ourselves. The result is that comedy and personal affirmations become a part of the worship experience and an accent is placed on God's love to the exclusion of His law. Hence, worship becomes performance and Christian youth ministry activities generally strive to become 'happenings' or 'events.' This is evident in the hyperbole now generally associated with the promotion of youth ministry activities.

When youth ministry activities are viewed as happenings or events, they are no longer anchored in the life-changing power of God's word. Instead, they reflect a trust in the power of psychological techniques, especially those relating to large-scale entertainment events, to influence individuals and to create group identification. The result is that youth ministry often becomes little more than therapeutic intervention. I have personally witnessed the use of known psychological techniques by youth ministers in a youth worship service. No mind control technique, including any technique embedded in Neuro-Linguistic Programming interventions, has any place in youth ministry. Such techniques are not only contrary to the gospel and quite dangerous but also a severe breach of the fiduciary responsibility that youth ministers owe to parents and youth.

The emphasis on form rather than content means that constant change becomes necessary to hold the attention of young people whose fundamental needs remain unaddressed. The failure of such programs to help youth to access the real source of power for change is reflected in the proliferation of "power" ministries for youth and the hype associated with their promotion. If a youth ministry activity is helping to introduce a young person to Christ, it does not need to maintain a constant level of excitement or novelty.

One of the consequences of the shift from content to form in youth ministry programs is that many contemporary approaches to youth ministry now integrate stage theories of moral or spiritual development in their planning processes. Stage theories suggest that humans develop through a number of stages in an invariant order. Therefore, experiences are graded to allow young people to progress through each of these stages. Like all theories that are based upon a humanistic understanding of human behavior, stage theories of moral or spiritual development deny the power of the gospel to transform the life.

One theorist who has exercised influence upon Christian youth ministry is Lawrence Kohlberg. His six-stage theory of moral development is not unlike the New Age concept of stages of enlightenment. Interestingly, both humanists and New Age devotees share a commitment to the ascent of man. Humanists perceive mankind evolving to a higher state of being while those committed to the New Age see mankind evolving to a higher state of consciousness, namely godhood. Both share common ground in the value of group processes to facilitate change. That is why encounter or discussion groups are popular in youth ministry. Instead of focusing on the word of God, leaders introduce group discussions of moral or spiritual dilemmas to promote development.

The Bible says that there is only one way (John 14:6). The New Age says that there are many ways and that there is good in every voice. While it is true that Jesus, as the true light, lightens every man who comes into the world, truth can be rejected. Hence, those who do not speak in accordance with what God reveals are not to be accepted as safe guides. It is the New Age that has encouraged the revival of ancient spiritualism. Encounter groups encourage practices that are common to shamanism and should be avoided at all times. Discussion groups that encourage young people to think that their opinions are a safe guide to decision-making will ultimately lead to the adoption of spiritualistic practices. Personality typing, leadership profiling and other developments in humanistic psychology ultimately lead in the same direction. They take the focus off God's transforming power and lead people to find the power to change in New Age practices. The way of salvation is only through Christ.

The result of adopting practices grounded in the New Age movement and humanistic psychology is the replacement of the absolute standards of the Bible with the prevailing cultural standards, which are determined by the thinking of the age. Movies, rock music, social and disco dancing, jewelry and make-up, things that are condemned by Biblical principles, become not only an acceptable part of Christianity but are considered in some cases to be indispensable modes of communication in the modern world. Taking on the role previously given to the Bible, popular culture becomes the arbiter of what is acceptable within Christianity and the mediator of its truths. The changeable nature of popular culture means that there are no fixed reference points to determine what is right or wrong. The true order is rapidly inverted and good become evil and evil appears good. Reproof directed to the adoption of inappropriate cultural practices is interpreted as criticism and those who counsel a return to Biblical principles are seen as relics of a less enlightened age.

Yet, the Bible is very clear that the old paths contain the good way (Jeremiah 6:16). In a changing world, change becomes inevitable. There is nothing inherently wrong with innovation. However, innovation must always remain within the boundaries that the Lord establishes. For example, forms of dress may change over time but the principles of modesty and distinction between the sexes remain. As long as the church is careful to adopt only those practices that are consistent with timeless principles, there is safety. But let the principle be established that social norms can be adopted without reference to what God has revealed in the Bible and the sure result will be a dangerous groupthink that sees light where there is only darkness and chaos.

Addictions

A great deal of time, energy and money is expended in trying to deal with the drug problem in our world today. Programs, whether preventative or ameliorative in focus, seem to have limited success. At its base, drug taking is a problem stemming from lack of self-control. A drug addiction therefore demands a spiritual solution. Yet, there are practices, some of which are prevalent in youth ministry, that encourage drug addiction and other addictive behaviors. The presence of a single addiction in the life opens the door to other forms of addictive behaviors. Hence, it is important to give due attention to the potential antecedents of drug taking.

We are to glorify God in our bodies. Yet, Christians routinely consume tea, coffee, colas and chocolate, all of which are addictive. If we want to encourage mastery of the appetites and passions, we must be careful to bring all of our practices into line with the Biblical principle of temperance. We should not encourage the consumption of food or drink that may lead to an addiction to tobacco, alcohol or drugs. We must also be careful to avoid using or giving implicit approval to practices that may not been seen in the same terms as drugs but which are still addictive and very destructive. Two things that fall into this category are rock music and movies.

The grave danger of rock music is its direct association with the drug culture. The driving beat subdues the rational faculties and opens the door to sensual indulgences of all kinds. Movies blur the boundaries of reality and the imagination and encourage a focus on the self. In combination, addictive practices are even more destructive. No one is truly free while one addiction is present in the life. Anything that breaks down self-control is to be avoided.

Ironically, the emphasis on developing self-esteem in many youth ministry programs works against those who may be struggling with addiction. Self-esteem is an artificial and undue regard for the self. Its development leads to pride and self-sufficiency and a focus on feelings and selfish desires. Young people do not need self-esteem; they need conversion. With conversion comes true humility and true self-development. Conversion enables a person to develop their talents and abilities for service to God and to others in a way that avoids the pitfalls of pride and self-serving.

Another highly destructive addiction that may be encouraged by some youth ministry promotional practices is gambling. Lucky door prizes and draws are an expression of the gambling impulse. In relation to the issue of addiction, it needs to be recognized that addiction can operate even before there is a staking of money. It is the element of chance in combination with the prospect of a material or other benefit that is addictive to the imagination. Thus, lucky door prizes, draws and other promotional devices that distribute rewards by chance may stimulate a psychological addiction to gambling even before a person engages in the act of gambling. The same may apply to all games of chance because winning is attractive for many people even when there is no material benefit involved.

The significance of the distribution of material rewards by chance can be seen most clearly in the powers attributed to Fortuna, the Roman goddess of chance or lot. Originally a bearer of prosperity and increase, Fortuna became identified with the goddess of chance known to the Greeks as Tyche, but retained her association with the bounty of the soil and fertility.[3] Fortuna personified the idea that much of what happens in life is due to chance (Murray 1988, 182). She is often depicted with a rudder to indicate that she is the controller of destinies and a cornucopia to show that she is the source of abundance. Sometimes she is depicted standing on a ball or associated with other devices that indicate the uncertainty of fortune.

In 1995, I visited the Vatican Museum in Rome. I noticed there a statue of Fortuna holding a rudder in her right hand and a cornucopia in her left hand. The symbolism of the rudder and cornucopia reveals that Lady Fortuna or Lady Luck usurps the prerogatives that belong to God alone. It is God who is in control of the destiny of mankind (Daniel 2:20-22). Our personal destiny is not subject to chance but to choice and the Bible associates our choice of God with the temporal benefits of life and longevity (Deuteronomy 30:19, 20). As our choice of God determines our destiny, it also places the responsibility for our prosperity in God's hands. It is God's prerogative to provide us with temporal blessings (Psalm 34:10; 84:11).

Thus, when people engage in the distribution of material benefits by chance, they are paying homage to Lady Fortuna. Similarly, in rolling dice, people pay homage to Tyche; for legend has it that the first set of dice was dedicated to her.[4] Distributing benefits by chance is a repudiation of God's sovereignty and beneficence. The use of chance in youth ministry demonstrates a lack of trust in God's power to order the affairs of mankind and to exercise due diligence in the care and protection of those who choose Him.

If those responsible for youth ministry were to conduct an audit of their practices most would find that they are unwittingly contributing to the problem of addictive behaviors among the young. We tend to be alarmed by drugs. Yet, drugs are only the tip of a much larger iceberg of addictive behaviors that reside in youth culture. Youth need help to resist these pressures. They need to be shown how they can keep their hearts single to the glory of God in every aspect of their lives.

Notes
[1] Stories Worth Re-Reading, Ithaca, Angela's Bookshelf, 1992.
[2] Britannica DVD 2000, Earrings.
[3] Britannica DVD 2000, Fortuna.
[4] Britannica DVD 2000, Tyche.

Chapter 5

WANDERING STARS

Farewell to Reason

The makeover of youth ministry is not the result of random changes to longstanding practices. There is a discernible direction to the changes and it is a direction that appears desirable to many. Yet, the underlying ideas behind this change in direction are rarely made explicit. It is because these ideas are seldom brought to the surface and examined closely that the practices that flow from them seem reasonable. When the ideas that sustain the present revolutionary changes to youth ministry are compared with the teachings of the Bible, a serious conflict emerges.

Christians are to have sound reasons for the hope that is in them and the practices that this hope enjoins upon them (1 Peter 3:15). These reasons must be defensible for they are to be an acceptable answer to those who enquire about our hope. That means that the answers given to an enquiry must recommend themselves to the enquirer on rational grounds. They must pass the test of public defensibility (2 Peter 1:20). What type of reason qualifies on these grounds? How can the reasons for our hope appear sound to an enquirer? How can we ensure that our practices are soundly based and that they will recommend themselves to an honest enquirer? The Bible provides the answers to these questions.

Jesus revealed in an exchange with the scribes and Pharisees that reason serves the orientation of the heart (Luke 5:22). In other words, reasoning is contingent or dependent; it is not absolute. The mind serves the desires and choices. That is why the disciples were not able to comprehend fully the mission of Jesus before the crucifixion. Their desire for supremacy blinded them to the spiritual nature of the kingdom that Jesus came to establish. It was only when their hearts were broken and subdued that they received clear spiritual discernment. It is the same today.

Spiritual discernment is the result of willingness to follow all the revealed counsel of God (John 7:17). That means that a willingness to be guided by the Bible in all matters of belief and practice is the foundation of true spiritual discernment. If so, it is to be expected that those who refuse to do the will of God will be left without discernment. Human traditions that deny the authority of the commandments of God bring vanity and blindness to human thinking (Matthew 15:9). Those who refuse to love the truth that God graciously reveals to them will eventually be deluded and believe lies.

God invites us to reason with Him in relation to the forgiveness and transformation that results from acceptance of the gospel (Isaiah 1:18). Reason aids the reception of truth but reason is not reliable unless it first accepts that which God reveals. We are then able to use reason to validate our choice of God when we accept God's invitation and see that God is indeed good. In other words, reason is necessary but not sufficient to comprehend truth. Yet, to enjoy the benefits that the gospel offers, we must be willing and obedient (Isaiah 1:19, 20). It is our willingness to follow all of God's revealed will that keeps us safe from spiritual delusion and truly sets us free.

It is the heart's response to the gospel that will determine the nature of our reasoning. We are what we think in our hearts (Proverbs 23:7). If we are to give sound answers to someone who asks us for the reasons for our hope, we can only do so if we first sanctify the Lord in our hearts. The Scriptures link the capacity for sound reasoning with a love for and obedience to the truth that God reveals. We are sanctified by God's word, which is truth (John 17:17). By corollary, we can only know the truth through God's word. That last point is of vital importance in dealing with issues that arise in youth ministry.

When Christians reason in accordance with the testimony of the Bible, their argumentation will be sound. The word of God is to guide us in all the practical decisions of life (Psalm 119:105). Even if we do not fully understand all the reasons why God enjoins a particular course of action upon us, we can know that there are good reasons why we should obey God's counsel in the matter. However, if the Bible is not permitted to explain itself, and there are attempts to impose human thinking upon the Biblical text or even to substitute human reason in its place, the certain result will be paralogical or illogical thinking.

All false reasoning begins with the rejection of God's revelation. Therefore, the false reasoning that is driving the destructive changes to youth ministry is indicative of the rejection of the authority of God's word. By rejecting clear Biblical principles, youth ministry descends into paralogy. Its thinking becomes almost indistinguishable from the paralogical thinking that pervades our postmodern world. Instead of drawing the world to the church, youth ministry simply opens the door for the world to flood into the church. The boundaries between good and evil become blurred and soon the true order is inverted and evil appears good. Most youth leaders are unaware that they have exchanged the Bible for their own imaginations.

Therefore, those who promote the thinking that is driving the bizarre changes to youth ministry today are wandering stars, with no fixed point of reference except their own imaginations (Jude 13). Their teachings lead into the blackness of eternal darkness. Those who follow these teachings will suffer the same end and it is therefore of vital importance that the ideas that are leading young people from the path of truth be exposed to the full light of day. Hence, the remainder of this chapter will be devoted to an examination of some of the most destructive concepts that are being promoted in youth ministry today.

Dominion Theology

One of the beliefs breaking down the barriers between the church and the world is dominion theology. That view argues that because God is supreme over all and because man has been given dominion over the earth, everything that happens in the world must be reclaimed for Him. Thus, such things as sports, theater, rock music, the arts and other expressions of popular culture should be reclaimed for God and made to serve His purposes. It is an attractive belief in a world that has marginalized the Christian contribution to culture. However, it is a belief that is Biblically unsound and profoundly incoherent.

It is true that God is supreme over all, and that man was originally given dominion over all the earth, but it is also true that Satan has challenged God's supremacy throughout the universe. The fall of mankind made Satan the prince of this world. Satan claims dominion over the earth (Matthew 4:8-11). The plan of salvation is designed to recover the world and its people from Satan's grip and to bring security to the universe. Yet, while Satan has already been judged, he remains at large and is working to deceive the whole world. Satan and his angels work especially to deceive Christians to accept and promote his delusions. Yet, our Lord Jesus Christ is working to restore His complete dominion over the earth when the judgment of mankind is complete. The way is then open for the saints to have their legitimate dominion restored.

That means that while the controversy between good and evil rages in the universe, it is necessary for Christians to make due distinction between good and evil and between those who practice these opposing principles. Unless false teachings are exposed by the Bible, many will be led into fatal error. There is a dangerous belief that is gaining currency that something doesn't have to be good or bad, that there is neutral ground in the struggle between good and evil. While it is true that Biblical principles have to be implemented contextually, it is also true that Jesus does not leave us with neutral ground in relation to our commitment to Him or to the decisions that flow from this commitment. If good cannot be adequately distinguished from evil, then God is not just in judging us on this basis. The fact that He does so indicates that we must be careful to make proper judgments on Biblical grounds in relation to all innovations in youth ministry.

The flaw in the argument that Christians should reclaim and transform popular culture is revealed when dominion theology is taken to its logical conclusions. It means that Christians would be obliged to accept responsibility for transforming things, such as bars, night clubs and casinos that clearly breach Christian principles. Yet, to exercise dominion in a Christian sense in these cases is to seek their abolition and that means that they no longer retain their defining characteristics. In other words, if these things are not acceptable as they stand, it means that there are some things in popular culture that are inconsistent with Biblical principles and cannot be integrated into Christian culture without destroying their characteristics. Once it is admitted that such a distinction must be made, something that can only be determined by the Bible, it means that Biblical principles are paramount. When the Bible is paramount, anything that does not comply with its principles, and is not transformable without changing its essential nature, is to be avoided.

Apply these insights to rock music and it becomes clear that rock is not transformable without changing its essential nature. If its essential nature is retained, it can never be acceptable. If Christians adopt this form of popular culture, we should therefore expect that it would be the Christians who are conformed to rock music and not the other way around. That is exactly what we do find. The same applies to sports, theater and other manifestations of popular culture. The argument that Christians are exercising dominion when they engage in the manifestations of popular culture that are essentially incompatible with the Bible cannot therefore be sustained. Thus, one of the ways that we can test the validity of concepts is to extend them to their logical conclusions and see if an absurdity appears.

Chronological Snobbery

We have been conditioned by more than a century of evolutionary proselytizing and technological innovation to think that the passage of time automatically produces progress. The modern world is changing so rapidly that innovation seems desirable. The pressure for change and innovation is ever present to the extent that change and novelty are now usually considered good in themselves. The result is largely what C. S. Lewis called "chronological snobbery," which is the uncritical acceptance of something just because it is modern.

Yet, many of the things that are considered innovative today in youth ministry are really only outmoded concepts dressed up in new packages. There is nothing new under the sun. Progress can only be measured against some fixed evaluative standard. In the spiritual and moral domains, the Bible is that fixed standard. If Biblical standards of evaluation are discarded, change will unavoidably result in confusion and defeat. The disastrous result of the infatuation with novelty is evident early in sacred history. Eve was seduced by new and exciting concepts. In embracing these ideas, Eve exercised her own reason and senses independently of God's instruction. We live with the consequences today.

The history of God's dealings with mankind in the Bible is replete with examples of how individuals and groups tried to do things their own way and brought confusion, weakness and defeat upon themselves. In the time of the Judges, every man did that which was right in his own eyes. When Judah was in rebellion in the time of Jeremiah, God used Jeremiah to articulate a concept that is just as relevant today as when it was written more than two thousand years ago. The people of Judah were crying peace when there was no peace. They were committing abominations and had lost all sense of shame. To deal with this situation, God spoke through Jeremiah to the people. He told them to look back in their history for the good paths that had previously been revealed to them (Jeremiah 6:16). They were told that they were to walk in these paths and that, in so doing, they would find rest for their souls.

The great lesson here is that solutions to the dilemmas of contemporary youth ministry are to be found in the timeless principles of God's word. We need to obey God's counsel. There is an important place for innovation in youth ministry but innovation must always remain within the boundaries laid down in God's word. There is a general lack of knowledge of the Biblical principles of youth ministry and young people's lives are being destroyed by this ignorance (Hosea 4:6). Instead of asking counsel of God, many who are involved as youth leaders are following the ideas of secular thinkers who have no sympathy with Christianity.

The new youth ministry rejects the notions of conformity and respectability. It marches to the beat of its own drum. It rejects previous boundaries that have divided Christianity from the world and crosses the safety lines that God has established to protect His young people from harm. The new youth ministry takes pride in its contrast with previous approaches to youth ministry and its courage in withstanding criticism. It is challenging and impatient and believes that there is a pressing need for youth to change the church before the church becomes completely irrelevant to the needs of modern society. Doctrine and theology are seen as marginal to the question of relevance.

However, the focus on relevance has not produced ideas and practices in youth and young adult ministry that will prepare young people for the challenges and duties of adult life. In fact, it seems to lock young people into a way of thinking and behaving that makes it almost impossible for them to relate to adults in the church and to make the shift to a mature form of faith. The old forms of conformity are simply replaced by new forms of conformity. The canons of popular culture become the new orthodoxy. It is extremely difficult to reclaim youth who have been shaped by these radical changes. Their capacity for reasoning, their tastes and their attitudes seem to be permanently affected.

When a church permits its young people to become bound to the prevailing culture, it is assisting its own disintegration. Popular culture is moving away from Biblical morality. Having established a precedent, will the church move with popular culture when it goes lower in the scale of morality? Will it be possible to reverse directions in the future? Will it be easier for youth and adults to find common cause in the unity of the faith? Youth who have been encouraged to question and criticize their churches are not going to be particularly amenable to correction. Some young people are already defiant and aggressive when their practices are questioned.

True engagement with popular culture challenges its intellectual base and the evolutionary worldview that sustains it (Revelation 14:6, 7). True cultural engagement is not to adopt the maxims and fashions of popular culture but to place the everlasting gospel in its historical and prophetic context and to contrast it with the nihilism and despair that pervades the West. It is not engagement with culture simply to accommodate to it. That is neither creative nor defensible. Also, let it never be forgotten that the last warning messages that go to the nations of earth include messages that warn against the dangers of false and apostate religion (Revelation 14:8-11). These messages are to go everywhere within Christianity where false doctrine is held. Therefore, a religion that downplays doctrine and Biblical standards of living is not a religion that has any relevance to the modern world.

A Matter of Taste

One of the ideas that is gaining currency in youth ministry is that a young person's selection of music, recreational activities, and dress styles is simply a matter of taste and that whatever is selected needs to be respected. It is suggested that our tastes are largely determined by our upbringing and what we are accustomed to and that our tastes and preferences are not a matter of importance. However, the Bible is quite clear that there is to be a distinction between the unconverted and converted lifestyle (1 Peter 2:20, 21). Biblical principles do not forbid individuals from exercising their legitimate preferences within acceptable limits but even our preferences must be sanctified so that whatever we choose fitly represents Christ.

There are many Christians today who have rejected rock music and its variants because they recognize from their knowledge of the Bible and personal experience that these forms of music are not compatible with their commitment to Christ. They did not give up these forms of music because they disliked them. Many were deeply attracted to them and had to struggle to retrain their tastes to appreciate musical forms that were previously alien to them. The same struggle is often evident in other areas of their lives. That is particularly the case in relation to clothes and adornment for this is the area of our lives in which self asserts itself most readily. Thus, many who object to the beat music and the casual dress at worship services are not doing so because they dislike these things or have never felt attracted to them but simply because they have been delivered from the grip of these obsessions and understand the dangers they pose to the Christian life.

Worship is one of the areas in which personal taste is currently being defended most strongly. Yet, from the beginning, God has been very specific in relation to how we are to approach Him in worship. God instructed Cain and Abel that they were to approach Him through an animal offering. Rejecting this instruction, Cain thought that his offering of produce would be acceptable. God refused to accept the offering. There was an important symbolism in the animal sacrifice in that it pointed forward to the sacrifice of Jesus Christ, the Lamb of God. God has reasons for the specific instructions that He gives to mankind and it is important that we obey His instructions.

Within a brief period of the giving of the Ten Commandments on Mount Sinai, the Israelites approached Aaron to make them a golden calf. The Israelites were familiar with the worship of the calf in Egypt and, although God had forbidden idol worship, the golden calf was soon set up and worshipped as their deliverer. The worship of the calf was mingled with the worship of the Lord. God described the actions of the Israelites as a corruption of the true worship that He had instituted among them (Exodus 32:7).

As Joshua and Moses descended to the camp of Israel, Joshua, after hearing the shouting of the people in the camp, commented to Moses that there was the noise of war in the camp (Exodus 32: 17). Moses, having being alerted by the Lord, replied that it was not the noise of war but of singing. The worship of the golden calf had produced a loud, raucous form of singing that was similar to the noise of war. The parallel with the rock music that has invaded Christianity today is too obvious to be missed.

However, the parallels with today do not finish with the music of the Israelites as they worshipped the golden calf. When Moses reached the camp, the Israelites were dancing naked around the calf (Exodus 32:19, 25). They had abandoned themselves to the dissolute practices of the heathen religions that pervaded the region. Now it was Moses' turn to be offended and he broke the tables of the Ten Commandments upon which God had written His commandments with His own finger. That act indicated to the Israelites that they had broken the covenant that God had made with them. It was only with the severest action that Moses was able to stay the awful rebellion that had broken out among the

Israelites.

The lessons from that fearful apostasy are relevant to those who live in the period just before the end of the world (1 Corinthians 10:11, 6). Those who do not hold to true worship in the last days will inevitably worship the beast and his image (Revelation 14:9). When Paul warned the Corinthians about the dangers of apostasy, he drew attention to the actions of the Israelites that were associated with their worship of the golden calf. Christians today must guard their worship practices from all forms of apostasy and they must uphold the principles of true recreation and modesty that help protect against immorality. How we dress for worship and the music we use in approaching God is important. Our untutored tastes in these matters can never be the criteria for determining what is acceptable to God.

Christianity is about self-denial and following Jesus. The true Christian is known by the fruits of his or her life. Selfish inclinations and improper tastes and affections are to be relinquished. God does not desire to make life miserable for those who give themselves to Him. Jesus came to give us life and to give it more abundantly (John 10:10). In His great love and mercy, God prohibits only those things that war against our souls (1 Peter 2:11).

From the Heart

The idea that personal or group tastes in religious matters are always to be respected is invariably accompanied by the belief that it is not what we do but the motive behind the action that is important. In other words, if we do things from the heart our sincerity sanctifies our actions and makes them acceptable to God. Our worship is then authentic worship regardless of how we choose to do it. That idea is used to justify the actions of individuals or groups who wish to worship or serve God in accordance with their own preferences.

God tells us through Jeremiah that the heart is deceitful above all things and desperately wicked and that only He can know it (Jeremiah 17:9). So it is clear that we need to see our hearts as God sees them. Sincerity can never convert error into truth. Repetition can never convert error into truth. Only the truth sanctifies and truth is to be found in God's word. Jesus always obeyed His Father's commandments. God's law was within His heart. That is why the new or converted heart leading to obedience figures prominently in both the Old and New Testaments. Hence, doing something from the heart is no guarantee that it will be acceptable to God.

The Bible contains some well-known examples of that fact. Paul persecuted the early church with great zeal and sincerity of purpose but he was still badly wrong. Uzzah's motive in touching the Ark of the Covenant was no doubt good but his action was presumptuous disobedience to God's instruction that the ark was not to be touched. God saw that Uzzah's heart was not right with Him. Such a brazen act of public defiance against God could not be allowed to pass unpunished. Uzzah's death is a reminder that God is particular.

If the ark had been transported by the sons of Kohath, in accordance with God's instructions, Uzzah would not have been put in such danger. David reasoned that it was acceptable to transport the Ark of the Covenant by ox cart because the Philistines had done so without penalty. Yet, the Philistines had acted in ignorance of God's instruction and God did not hold them accountable. It was the light that had been shed upon Israel that brought guilt. God had instructed the Israelites how the ark was to be transported and they could not claim ignorance.

And so it is with Christians today in relation to God's requirements concerning worship. Christians have the Bible and the witness of sacred history to inform their actions. There is no excuse for ignorance of God's instructions and those who persist in disobedience will inevitably reap what they have sown. No excuse will be heard on the day when every knee bows before Christ and every tongue confesses that He is Lord. We must worship God not only in spirit but also in truth (John 4:23).

Those who believe that anything done from the heart is acceptable to God often elevate relationship with God above obedience to Him. But it is important to note that God does not recognize the existence of a relationship where professed Christians disobey Him (Matthew 7:21-23). While it is not the cause of salvation, obedience is a condition of salvation (Romans 2:13). God accepts us when we come to Him in repentance. But God does not leave us where He finds us. He knows that sin is the cause of human misery and He desires to separate from sin those who come to Him in repentance. He desires to transform their lives. That is why God inspires so much counsel in regard to the way we are to approach Him and the relationships we are to have with others. Hence, a true relationship with God always results in obedience to Him (Revelation 14:12).

Despite the clear witness of the Bible, many young people today are encouraged to believe that they need make no effort to bring themselves up to a higher standard, a more elevated life of obedience and service to God. The line of distinction is not drawn clearly between the young Christian and the world and the result is a form of Christianity that is often indistinguishable from the world. While there is no clear distinction between Christianity and the world that it renounces, young people will find it extremely difficult to make a complete surrender to God or to make any real impact on a world that desperately needs to hear the gospel of the saving and transforming power of Jesus Christ.

There's Good in Every Voice

One of the reasons why Christians are so accommodating of change and diversity in youth ministry today is because of the belief that there is good in every voice. This translates into the maxims that all ways are good and that we can each worship God in our own way, resulting in some Christians changing the nature of God to suit their current enthusiasms. In essence, such thinking blends seamlessly with the New Age movement.

In an age when self-expression is considered a right, these beliefs and maxims are extremely popular and they tend to be difficult to counter because they take their adherents outside the realm of reason. However, there are strong reasons why the whole package of beliefs must be rejected. While it is true that there is good in every voice, it does not necessarily follow that every voice is good. No person is completely devoid of some truth for everyone born into the world is given some opportunity to know truth. But the real issue is not whether a person has some truth but whether they have *the* truth. Jesus said, "I am the way, the truth, and the life: no man cometh unto the Father, but by me" (John 14:6).

The fact that Jesus is *the* way, the truth and the life does not preclude the use of different methods in youth ministry that are consistent with the principles of the Bible. But it does mean that there is no room for philosophies of youth ministry that are denied by Biblical teachings. Logically, as well as Biblically, that is the case. For example, when Jesus said that He was the way, He excluded every other philosophy from having the least particle of merit in relation to salvation. If what Jesus said is true, which we know to be the case, there is no other way to salvation. However, even if Jesus' statement is false, which it is manifestly not, it disconfirms the belief that all ways are good because at least in this one instance a way that is claimed to be true is false. It is such logical force that gives added power to Jesus' claim to represent the only way to salvation.

Therefore, if Jesus is the only way, it follows that any way that is not consistent with His teachings must be rejected. It is not possible, then, to argue that all ways of youth ministry are good. It also follows that there are not multiple philosophies of worship that are consistent with Biblical teachings. As we noted in the previous section, we must choose only those forms of worship that conform to the spirit and truth of Christianity. That conclusion is confirmed by the counsel of Paul to Timothy in which Timothy was exhorted to, "Preach the word; be instant in season, out of season; reprove, rebuke, exhort with all longsuffering and doctrine" (2 Timothy 4:2). Clearly, pluralism in religious matters, including forms of worship, is not part of God's plan.

While pluralism is the catch cry of modern youth ministry, it does not exist in reality. There are only two forms of worship. The first is that which conforms to the Biblical criteria. The second is that which doesn't conform to the Biblical criteria but which gives, by virtue of its complete contrast with the first, an impression of diversity. But if a close examination is made, the second form of worship is actually only a corruption of the first. It puts in place things that are not new and creative but only the worst forms of entertainment that the world has to offer. It is simply the overturning of the elevated principles of the Bible.

One of the reasons why so many pastors and youth ministry leaders today are so sensitive to reproof and rebuke in relation to the dreadful practices they condone is that error cannot stand in the presence of truth. When the light of Biblical truth is shed upon their unholy practices, they seek to denigrate the reprover rather than listen to the voice of reproof. In their response to the truth, they reveal that they do not truly believe in pluralism for they seek by every means to overturn true worship and to substitute their awful practices. "It is only your opinion," many retort, not seeming to realize that, if it is only a matter of opinion, your opinion is at least as good as the one they hold. It seems that such people are prepared to promote almost anything that God condemns but will not uphold that which He approves. Fortunately, we are not left in ignorance of what God desires.

The usual defense of those who fail to uphold their practices from Scripture is to change the nature of God so their practices are more consistent with the God of their own invention. The Deity of their imagination is accepting and nurturing and extremely tolerant. But when Moses asked to see God's glory, he was shown the seamless blend of mercy and justice that makes up the character of God (Exodus 34:5-7). Mercy is based upon love and justice is based upon law. So both love and law are part of God's character. Individuals may deny some aspect of God's character that does not fit with their desires but God is not thereby changed. Wishful thinking is a poor basis for sound belief.

What people are doing when they emphasize one aspect of God's character at the expense of another is to express the New Age concept that there can be different realities for different people. Unable to deal with issues in a Biblical fashion, such people retreat to an idiosyncratic or personal view of reality in which their view of God is just one among many acceptable views. Thus, the force of God's revelation of His own character is neutralized and the lifestyle consequences of accepting this revelation are marginalized. The barriers against false views of salvation and antinomianism are broken down. In the end, an eccentric form of Christianity subverts the true religion of Christ.

Relevance

The revolution in youth ministry has been sustained by the argument that change was necessary to bring the church more in line with contemporary youth culture. But what is the evidence that bringing the church closer to the world has resulted in greater success in retaining young people in the church or attracting secular youth to Jesus Christ? It seems that youth who have been subjected to the revolution are now almost totally secularized. They wear the same clothes as their secular counterparts. They listen to the same music. They speak the same language and they have the same interests. Their practice of Christianity is largely self-conscious and whimsical. There seems to be little to distinguish them from those who are not Christians. They have no real power to influence their culture because they have separated themselves from the true Source of their strength.

The attachment to rock music has created a group of young adults who find it extremely difficult to relate to older members of the church or even to each other. Many young adults in their thirties seem unable to make the transition from the youth culture to adult life. A significant part of their time that is devoted to association with other young adult Christians is concerned with rock music or sports. In some cases, these activities seem to define group identity. The church, once having approved the changes to youth ministry, is left with an awful dilemma. If it does not continue the current direction, it seems to face a crisis, for many young people now have no taste for Biblical modes of worship or evangelism. On the other hand, if the current directions are pursued much longer, the future viability of the church is undermined.

Some perceive the solution to this dilemma to be the transplantation of the youth worship style into adult worship. Hence, efforts have been made at the congregational level and at church conventions to impose the youth worship style upon mature believers. The distinction between right and wrong and acceptable and unacceptable ways to worship is blurred by a terminological innovation in which, for example, the change may be characterized as a move from a static to a dynamic form of worship. In an effort to accommodate youth, many adults accept this imposition upon their worship. The result, however, is a sense of powerlessness and bewilderment among older Christians. It does not seem to bother the sponsors of this compromise that the worship experience of mature adults is degraded by this compromise.

The willingness to corrupt adult worship exposes the poverty of the claim that youth worship is done in the name of authenticity. If authenticity is an important principle for youth worship, it must also be an equally important principle for adult worship. No spiritual leader has authority to introduce methods and practices that do not enjoy God's approval. The minds of the people are paralyzed by the noise and confusion and they are not able to make intelligent decisions in relation to their own eternal welfare. They are destroyed by a lack of knowledge. Meanwhile the failure of adults to resist the unwelcome changes simply delays corporate recognition that the rock music phenomenon is now out of control and cannot be subdued without massive fallout and dislocation.

True relevance is an intelligent and sensitive response to the genuine needs of people that emerge from the reality of sin in their lives and the lives of others. God has made provision to meet our needs in the plan of salvation and in the principles of evangelism and worship that have been laid down in His word. The methods that are to be used in worship and evangelism are consistent with the God who reveals Himself in the Bible. There is to be perfect harmony between theology and method. Moses' experience at the burning bush reminds us that our God is holy and must be approached in a manner that reflects this fact. The solemnity of the sanctuary service reminds us that the house of God is to be treated with reverence. Our worship on this earth is to prepare us to worship a holy God in the courts above.

There are many people in our society, young and old, who are of refined and cultivated tastes. A degraded youth culture has no appeal to them and a Christian witness that comes to them clad in its garments is likely to cause them to turn away in revulsion. However, works that are consistent with true faith never repel but attract. Jesus is the light of the world and we can only be the light of the world as we imitate His faith and His works. As we draw closer to Jesus, we draw the world closer to Him. Yet, if His image in us is destroyed by the adoption of cultural mores that are profoundly antagonistic to Him, we obscure His witness in the world.

There was a great falling away in the early centuries of the Christian era. It occurred because the church thought that by conforming its practices to the spirit of paganism it could influence pagans to join the church. To a great extent this strategy worked. Pagans poured into the church but they brought their superstitions with them. They never rose higher than the methods that had been used to win them to Christianity. In the end, paganism conquered Roman Christianity. The church was brought down to the level of pagan superstition and idolatry. The mystery of iniquity was working in the time of the apostles but was largely restrained while they were alive. After their death, the purity of the apostolic faith was gradually compromised. Foreseeing this, Paul exhorted the Thessalonians to hold fast to the things that had been revealed to them (2 Thessalonians 2:15). We would do well to heed this counsel today in relation to youth ministry.

Chapter 6

FACING THE CRISIS

Group Think

The adoption of the principle of cultural relevance has brought youth ministry to a state of profound crisis. God's plan of separation from the world and obedience to all of His instruction is almost universally rejected. The line of demarcation between Christianity and the world is no longer distinct and the idols of popular culture are now firmly established in the affections of a generation of Christian youth. The effects are being felt in the church at large as the changes in youth ministry destabilize the historic practices of Biblical Christianity. Unless this crisis is addressed resolutely, it will result in the spiritual destruction of countless young people and gravely injure the cause of God.

In any crisis, the first step towards its resolution is to recognize the nature and extent of the problem. Unfortunately, a significant part of the crisis is the loss of reason that accompanies the practices that have been adopted. Youth ministry leaders cannot enthusiastically use sports, theater and rock music in their programs without losing the Biblical perspectives that undergird spiritual discernment. That, in turn, makes it impossible for them to critically evaluate their programs. When their programs fail to achieve lasting spiritual results, which must invariably be the case, the deepening problems are identified as an inadequate application of change. Most youth leaders feel that the solution is to move even closer to the prevailing youth culture.

Should some youth ministry leaders entertain doubts about their current directions, there are a number of factors that discourage a return to forms of ministry that meet Biblical criteria. First, there is the peer pressure that punishes any departure from the prevailing orthodoxy. It takes courage to admit a mistake and to advocate the roll back of practices that have become firmly established in the denominational and ecumenical contexts. Second, there is the resistance of young people who have become comfortable with exercising their inclinations and tastes without restraint. Once released from proper restraints, many young people do not desire more disciplined forms of worship and evangelism. Third, youth ministry leaders who reject the new orthodoxy endanger their employment prospects or their leadership positions for they find themselves out of step with the majority.

If a youth leader manages to overcome these constraints, there is still the issue of the entrenched theology that drives the changes. There is a close and decided relationship between theology and practice. Changing practice usually means also a change of theology. A return to a Biblical conception of youth ministry means the prospect of a continuing struggle with forces that are not sympathetic to this perspective. Thus, the counter-revolution in youth ministry has some very difficult obstacles to overcome. It is easier to quieten the nagging doubts and to run with the majority.

The Bible is replete with examples of group think and its devastating consequences. A particularly apposite example for today's world is the experience of the Antediluvians just prior to the flood. They ignored the warning messages of Noah for they were convinced that Noah was an alarmist and that there was no real reason for concern. The Bible tells us that a parallel form of group think will possess the world before Jesus comes the second time (Luke 17:26-30). The crisis that precedes the end of the world is a religio-political crisis in which almost the whole religious world is drawn into a confederacy against God (Revelation 13:11-17). That is able to occur because God's professed people have largely rejected His requirements.

Youth leaders who encourage a love of the world in young people by incorporating sports, theater and rock music in their programs are playing an important role in preparing them for the end-time deceptions of Satan. It is unlikely that the greater majority of youth leaders or young people will recognize this until it is too late to rectify the situation. Yet, all who have a love of youth and who have a correct knowledge of the principles of youth ministry must continue to make their voices heard. While reason is powerless against a strong delusion, the Holy Spirit can use sanctified reason to reach those who are still open to His appeals.

What then can be done to alert youth leaders and young people to the dangers of unsanctified entertainments and amusements in worship, nurture and evangelism in these last days? It is not enough to know the dangers that various practices pose to the spiritual health of young people. It is also necessary for concerned church members, parents and young people to articulate a defensible alternative to the prevailing orthodoxy. That means that all advocates for reform should have a clear understanding of Biblical principles of youth ministry and be able to identify and promote sound ideas and practices. Accordingly, the remaining sections of this chapter will address Biblical principles of youth ministry, sound alternatives to prevailing practices and the principles of effective advocacy.

Biblical Principles of Youth Ministry

The most important need that young people have today is the need of conversion and submission to God. "Remember now thy Creator in the days of thy youth" is God's injunction to youth, coming down to us from ancient times (Ecclesiastes 12:1). A young life that is not under God's control is vanity. God judges the young for their willful disregard of his commandments and for giving free reign to their own desires (Ecclesiastes 11:9, 10). Everyone must give account to God, including youth. It is important, then, that the focus of youth ministry is the plan of salvation. Ongoing counsel and support should be provided to youth to help them grow spiritually and to become effective disciples. Youth should be enlisted in evangelism and, because of their inexperience, will have special needs for training in proclaiming the gospel.

Every aspect of youth ministry must be directed to upholding the plan of salvation and producing effective young disciples for Christ. What type of ministry and what class of practices will produce this outcome? The answer is clearly spelled out in the Bible. "Deep calleth unto deep" writes the Psalmist (Psalm 42:7). Only those directions and practices that assist youth to respond from the depths of their hearts to the depths of God's call to them are legitimate. Approaches and activities that leave youth with their affections partly in the world and partly with God will produce a superficial religious experience that will hinder them from responding to "the deep things of God" (1 Corinthians 2:10).

The carnal mind is at enmity against God. It is hostile to God and must be transformed and renewed. Only the indwelling Spirit is able to keep the mind in a state of renewal. The transformed mind, however, is no longer conformed to the world. Yet, it can remain transformed only so long as it refuses to be conformed to the world. When the boundaries between carnality and renewal are blurred in youth ministry by the introduction of worldly practices, the mind will adapt most readily to the worldly practices. The mind rises no higher than the lowest thing that it is prepared to contemplate and accept. It is most important, then, that youth ministry practices are consistent with the fundamental objectives of facilitating and maintaining discipleship among young people.

That means that all practices that diminish the higher faculties of mind, wisdom and discernment among youth will work against the restoration of God's image in their lives and thus against their spiritual interests. Even things as seemingly harmless as religious cartoons and jokes obscure the harsh reality of the conflict between good and evil and make it seem less upsetting and less important. In thinking about God's injunctions for His people to be sober minded, many make the mistake of equating this state of mind with a joyless existence. There is no incompatibility between a sober minded state and joyfulness. In fact, true joy is not possible in a light, frivolous atmosphere. Joy accompanies righteousness and peace (Romans 14:17).

God loves youth and will teach them if they are willing to obey Him (Psalm 71:17). God also has an important work for youth in the last days. Adults and youth will work together under the Holy Spirit to fulfill the Great Commission and finish God's work upon the earth (Acts 2:17). Unfortunately, youth ministry today tends to widen the gap between adults and youth. At a time when adults and youth need to be linked in bonds of mutual love, sympathy and understanding, youth are pulling away from adults with the approval of many youth leaders and spiritual leaders. The young are indulged with unsanctified worship, music, and amusements and made to feel that it is their right to these things, resulting in division and weakness.

However, young people are not to be despised. "Let no man despise thy youth," counseled Paul to the young Timothy (1 Timothy 4:12). God has a role for youth in the church and it is not to be denied to them. Yet, that role is not to draw away from adults and to seek to change things that have been established and vindicated through long experience. When Paul counseled Timothy in relation to his youth, he added, "be thou an example of the believers, in word, in conversation, in charity, in spirit, in faith, in purity." Youth are to take their legitimate place in the work of the church but it is not a place for immature faith or misplaced zeal.

There are some wonderful examples of what youth can accomplish for God in the Biblical stories of Samuel, Joseph, David, Isaiah, Jeremiah and Jesus, among others. Yet, there are also many experiences recorded about the devastating effects of unconverted youth who were given responsibilities for which they were not fitted. A particularly apposite example in relation to youth ministry is the story of the dividing of Israel after the death of Solomon. Rehoboam, Solomon's son, was made king. He was approached by Jeroboam, who had been the superintendent of the levy of forced labor under Solomon. Jeroboam presented the grievances of the people and indicated that the people were happy to serve Rehoboam but wanted a lightening of the load that they had to carry under Solomon's building program (1 Kings 12:3, 4).

Rehoboam took counsel of the old men who had been advisers to Solomon. They advised Rehoboam to make a generous and tactful response to the request of the people. Rehoboam rejected the counsel and sought another opinion from the young men who grew up with him and who were now in attendance at the court. Their counsel to him was that he should assert his authority and indicate to the people that their burden would be increased. Rehoboam took the unwise counsel and spoke harshly to the people, repeating the words that the young men had advised him to use. The result was a division between the northern tribes and the southern tribes of Judah. The division was never healed. The division of the tribes was one of the major turning points in sacred history.

While age is no guarantee of wisdom, Christian youth lack the experience to see issues as clearly as older Christians of sound faith and experience. A great mistake is made when the desires and opinions of unconverted and inexperienced youth are made the basis for youth ministry policy. Even the opinions of converted young people should be subjected to the wisdom of those of more mature experience. It is important that youth work closely with adults and that the relationship between youth and adults is based upon mutual respect.

In the context of mutual respect, older and more experienced

Christians should act as mentors to young people. As the story of John Mark reveals, young disciples sometimes make mistakes or fail in some important respect. John Mark's failure caused a sharp difference of opinion between Paul and Barnabas. John Mark responded positively to Barnabas' confidence in his potential and this story reveals the need for adults to take a sympathetic approach to the failures of young people and to give them opportunities to redeem mistakes. Paul later learned to appreciate John Mark (2 Timothy 4:11). The lesson here is that adults should involve young people and persevere with them.

Adult Christians should be sound examples to youth and should direct them to Christ and to righteous living. The power of example is very great and remains perhaps the most potent influence on young people. Youth will be more influenced by genuineness than by any other factor. The best-presented youth retention program will not suffice to hold many young people in the church if the reality does not match the rhetoric. Young people are generally highly idealistic and youth leaders make a mistake if they do not offer youth something that is worth their best energies.

In this context, it is extremely important that those who minister to youth ensure that they present all the counsel of God to them, just as Paul declared it to the Ephesian elders (Acts 20: 27). Paul also charged the Ephesian elders to do the same for the church over which they were overseers. Youth leaders are in a similar position of sacred trust. They must encourage young people in holy living. Youth who understand God's purposes for them will understand the challenge to study the word of God and implement it in every day life. Youth must be encouraged to take up this challenge in the power of the Holy Spirit. With such a group of young people, gimmicks and compromise will lose their appeal.

Youth ministry should place a high priority upon the provision of educational and training opportunities for young people to master the Scriptures. Paul systematically taught and defended the word of the Lord Jesus on a daily basis. While recreational activities are an important part of youth ministry programs, they should not be permitted to crowd out the study and appreciation of God's word. Many youth ministry programs are predominantly recreational in their focus. That is a mistake. Such programs send a very strong message that the Scriptures are less important than having a good time. They also reveal the fears of the leaders that they will not be able to hold the attention of the youth with a more spiritual focus. In the long term, programs with spiritual integrity will always be more effective than those which compromise with popular culture.

Where it can be done in good conscience, youth leaders should seek to draw close to those whom they are attempting to reach. Paul made himself all things to all men in order to save some (1 Corinthians 9:22). He did this for the gospel's sake. Yet, the principle is not without bounds. When Peter came to Antioch, Paul challenged him because he had changed his behavior and refused to eat with the gentiles when representatives of the circumcision party were present (Galatians 2:11-14). Paul did this because he believed that Peter's actions and the actions of other Jewish Christians, including Barnabas, were incompatible with the truth of the gospel. Thus, while we should seek to draw close to people, we must not make any inappropriate concessions to culture.

In relation to youth evangelism, the word of God must always remain the central focus. Youth leaders must preach, teach and prove it to young people, persuading them of its importance and testifying to its life changing power. It is not by the might of sophisticated and costly youth extravaganzas that youth will hear and respond to the gospel but in the faithful preaching of God's word attended by the quiet moving of the Holy Spirit.

Today, the tendency is to substitute theater and technology for the power of God's word, plainly and pointedly expressed. There is a tendency to get above the simplicity of the gospel and to despise more tried and proven methods of evangelism. All innovation in religious practice is to be consistent with the principles that God has revealed in His word. Innovation in youth ministry and evangelism is safe only as long as it retains the inspired focus on God's word, represents Jesus and the gospel appropriately and is faithful to the principles that God has revealed in His word.

Theater, rock music or its variants, and sports fail these criteria. They de-emphasize the word of God, misrepresent Christ's gospel and character and deface the image of God in man. The early Christians shunned pagan sports, theater and Dionysian music because of their religious origins and associations. Can we, who have full access to God's word and who are able to look back upon almost two thousand years of Christian history, not see the dangers in compromising with such practices today? Can we not see that adopting such practices in the name of enhancing the appeal of Christianity in the modern world will lead to the same dire consequences as when this policy was first implemented in the early centuries of Christianity?

The Biblical principles of youth ministry that have been outlined in this chapter are effective, for they are God's methods. They set the boundaries within which it is safe to operate. Leaders will not always do things in exactly the same way but that is not necessarily a disadvantage. Youth have the same fundamental needs but have different personalities. Therefore, there is some scope for variety within youth ministry. The important thing is to stay within the boundaries established by Biblical principles.

Adults can work for the best interests of youth when they love youth, recognize their potential and involve them wherever possible. They must provide consistent examples, act as mentors and guides, educate and train, and declare the whole counsel of God. Perseverance will be necessary and there should be no inappropriate concessions to culture. Whenever these principles are implemented consistently, the results will be astounding. If we want youth to be excited about the gospel, we must show them that we take its power seriously and are not willing to compromise its integrity. We must hold out to them a strong replacement for the prevailing secular youth culture.

A Place To Stand

The only valid philosophy of youth ministry is one that is totally derivable from the Bible. Therefore, in deciding what are sound alternatives to the prevailing practices in youth ministry, it is necessary to apply Biblical criteria. These criteria can be expressed as a series of questions. If positive answers to these questions can be given, the activity is safe. If no positive answer is forthcoming, the activity is unsafe. Let us note some of the important questions that help define defensible youth ministry.

First, will the activity bring us into a closer relationship with Christ? Sports, cinema, rock music and other similar manifestations of popular culture will not lead us to keep God in our thoughts. Participation in sports will not increase the desire to study God's word and to pray. It is impossible to feast on broadcast, cinematic or theatrical portrayals of fornication, adultery and other illicit human relationships without destroying our relationship with Christ. David allowed his mind to wander from the pathway of purity when he failed to discipline his eyes. Through his sin, he lost the relationship with God that he previously enjoyed and it was only through deep repentance that he was restored to favor with God (Psalm 51:10-12). The driving beat of rock music will not help us to draw closer to Christ in quietude and prayer. Youth need peace too.

If we are to have an eternal relationship with Christ, we must invest time and energy in building that relationship now. The things that draw our affections away from Christ must be discarded in order that we can cultivate eternity in our hearts. We lose nothing of any real value in complying with Biblical principles of Christian living. God never denies anything that is best for us to have. God's restrictions help us to clear the rubbish away from the door of eternity and to catch a vision of a better country. That is why a saving relationship with Christ will always lead to obedience to Him.

Second, will the activity promote the restoration of God's image in mankind? God created man in His own image but God's image in man has been defaced by sin. It is God's intention that His image be restored in fallen men through His transforming grace. That means that youth must receive the mind of Christ (Philippians 2:5). In receiving the mind of Christ, youth will become like Christ. Activities that divide youth and destroy their love, unity, humility and concern for others should be rejected. Competitive sports and activities fit this category and must be replaced with non-competitive alternatives. Theatrical manifestations, rock music and other forms of popular culture that destroy God's image in man will also be rejected.

Third, will the activity help youth to set their affections on heavenly things and give them a fitness for the society of heaven (Colossians 3:1-3). The human mind conforms to the things upon which it is permitted to dwell. If the minds of youth are encouraged to dwell upon the basest elements of youth culture, eternal realities will fade from view and their minds will be engrossed with that which is of no enduring value. Sports, theater, rock music and other manifestations of popular culture will not fit youth for the society of heaven.

The sports fan cannot enjoy heaven for it is a place without conflict. Mimes, magicians, actors, clowns and comedians cannot enjoy heaven for it is a place without defilement or pagan abominations. The worship of eternity is a holy worship. Only those who have cultivated a heavenly form of worship on earth will have the opportunity to worship God throughout eternity. God will not accept the worship of those who mingle the unholy with the holy. The rock enthusiast cannot enjoy heaven for it is a place of beautiful and elevating music. The mind-numbing and hypnotic beat of rock music will perish forever when Jesus comes again.

Fourth, will the activity develop the character attributes that every ambassador for Christ must have if he or she is to correctly represent Him? (2 Corinthians 5:20). Jesus, who is our example, never participated in the debasing games that were played in Palestine during the Roman occupation. He never led His disciples into extreme and dangerous sports and pastimes. His recreational time was spent apart with His disciples, gathering strength for the labor of the gospel. There is no record of Jesus' attendance at the theater. His music was simple and expressive (Matthew 26:30). If we are to be fitting representatives of Christ, we must live in accordance with the example He set us.

Fifth, will the activity encourage a proper stewardship of the physical and mental powers that have been entrusted to us? In the parable of the pounds, Jesus asks those to whom He entrusts resources to occupy until He comes (Luke 19:13). All who take the name of Christian are under sacred obligation to use the talents that they possess to extend the kingdom of heaven. Intelligence, energy, strength, skill, time and means are to be improved and devoted to the service of Christ. Will we work like Christ in unselfish service or will we like the Israelites in the wilderness eat and drink and rise up to play?

Sixth, and finally, will the activity improve relationships within families? God has promised that the Elijah message of the last days will turn the hearts of the fathers to the children and the hearts of the children to the fathers (Malachi 4:5, 6). Anything that divides families or widens inter-generational differences in the church is not part of God's plan for His people in the last days. When youth ministry becomes a point of tension in the church by introducing the rock beat in music, for example, it is certain that God is not in it.

Facing the Crisis

Youth ministry must focus on discipleship. It must direct youth to Christ and then empower them to serve Christ. The focus on entertainment that dominates youth ministry today denies the real needs of youth for meaning, purpose, challenge and accomplishment. Sports, theater, rock music and popular culture do not cater for these needs in any meaningful or lasting fashion. It is time to give youth experiences and opportunities that take account of their enormous potential in witnessing to the power of the gospel. Instead of encouraging alienation from adults, it is time to help youth to connect with the mission of the church and to accept adult responsibilities. When adults in their thirties are still not integrated into the church, but must have their own separate services and programs, it is a clear indication that youth ministry is not serving the wider needs of the church.

Effective youth ministry should cater for the spiritual, mental, physical and social needs of youth. In so far as it is possible, ministry to youth should be incorporated seamlessly into the wider church program. While it will be necessary to tailor some aspects of the program specifically for youth, youth ministry should help youth to connect with people of other age groups in the church. It is unwise to separate youth from adults for divine services. Integration into the wider church provides opportunities for service and personal growth. Youth can also take advantage of adult mentoring. Many adults have skills that youth need.

Camps and retreats, where the word of God is studied and God's works in nature are available for contemplation, are an important part of an effective youth ministry program. Camps and retreats take youth away from the sights and sounds of everyday life. There is an outlet for safe, enjoyable and constructive physical exercise. If competition is removed, natural bonding will take place and youth will be able to enjoy true fellowship and be refreshed in mind and spirit. Camps and retreats also provide an ideal venue for short training courses. Training courses should prepare youth to be involved in personal and corporate evangelism.

Youth should be taught to communicate the gospel in various ways to all age groups. It is important that youth understand the principles of soul winning. Voice training is also important for youth. The capacity to speak and sing correctly is of great value in conveying the gospel message. Youth should be taught principles of health and proper stewardship of their bodies. Biblical principles of dress, deportment and recreation should be taught along with instruction on interpersonal relationship and the responsibilities of marriage. The importance of the disciplined life, effective and efficient work, and true intellectual culture should be emphasized. Practical skills that can be used throughout life and which are particularly valuable in overseas missionary service should not be neglected.

Those who are involved in ministry to youth should express sympathy, affection and love for them. Youth leaders and mentors should be prepared to offer wise counsel and to help youth understand how they can be overcomers in the strength that the Lord provides. Yet, youth should never be indulged or permitted to openly express disrespect for adults. God requires youth to show due respect for those who are older in the faith. When the children mocked Elisha on his way to Bethel, the prophet's capacity to command the respect necessary for him to carry out his allotted tasks was threatened (2 Kings 2:23, 24). God's judgment upon the children indicates that those youth leaders who fail to correct disrespect for adults by youth or who actually encourage it by approving of expressions of immature judgment about church beliefs, practices and standards will one day have to render an account to God.

Reformation

The need for reformation in youth ministry is urgent. Yet, the beliefs and practices that have brought youth ministry and the church to crisis are firmly entrenched and will not be easily displaced. What can individuals or groups do to express their concerns and facilitate a reformation of youth ministry? While it is not possible to prescribe a course of action that will be suitable for every situation, there are some fundamental Biblical principles that apply in all circumstances.

The Bible states that if we want God to direct our paths, we must acknowledge Him in all our ways (Proverbs 3:6). Hence, we do not have the option of remaining silent when there is an issue of truth at stake. We are accountable to God for warning those who are turning aside from Him (Ezekiel 33:7-9). Those who do not come up to the help of the Lord are cursed (Judges 5:23). To be unconcerned and neutral in a religious crisis is to demonstrate antagonism to God.

What principles of action should determine how we discharge our duty to seek reformation of youth ministry? First, we need to understand that loyalty to God's counsel is the highest form of loyalty. When Peter and the other apostles were commanded not to speak in Jesus' name by the religious authorities, they enunciated this principle in these words, "We ought to obey God rather than man" (Acts 5:29).

Second, it must be understood that the person who reproves apostasy is not divisive. It is likely that the response to any attempt to reform youth ministry will be an attack on the person or group that raises the issues. Often such persons are labeled as divisive. Ahab accused Elijah of troubling Israel but Elijah turned the accusation back on Ahab because of his departure from the commandments of God and his worship of Baalim (1 Kings 18:17, 18).

Third, in addressing the issues in youth ministry, it is important to use light to dispel darkness (Isaiah 42:16). Error cannot stand where truth is clearly articulated. Fourth, the truth in relation to youth ministry should be spoken in love (Ephesians 4:15). Reformers should be careful not to unnecessarily antagonize. Fifth, it is important for reformers not to be easily discouraged. Error, apostasy and rebellion have no moral strength and those who challenge it should remember that God will sustain them (Ezekiel 3:8, 9). Sixth and finally, it is important to take the long-term view when difficulties seem to prevail for we can do nothing against the truth, but for the truth (2 Corinthians 13:8).

There are many accountability mechanisms that exist in the church and it is important to use all of them in addressing youth ministry issues. In the local church, you should begin with youth leaders themselves but, if no satisfactory response is forthcoming, it will be necessary to speak to the pastor and elders. If a satisfactory response is still not forthcoming, the next step is to express your concerns to the church board, either personally or in writing. The final step in the local church is to have your concerns discussed at the church business meeting. Have the matter placed on the agenda and move a motion as this creates an opportunity for action and resolution and also provides a right of reply for the mover.

If your concerns are a wider problem in the church, it will be necessary to address them as a systemic matter. The same principles of accountability apply at the wider level. Always be specific in identifying your concerns and always follow through as it sends strong signals that you are serious in your intentions. It is essential that those who share common concerns express these concerns collectively. Those who are speaking out should be supported. But it is also necessary to guard credibility by the way in which actions are taken. The spirit in which something is presented is very important to the possibility of a successful outcome. Constant prayer will be an important part of maintaining a calm and constructive approach.

Epilogue
Events in the world indicate that the coming of Jesus Christ is at hand. Already, there have been moves to circumscribe civil

freedoms in the name of security. The ease with which this has taken place and the rapidity with which a worldwide confederacy has been put in place to confront the threat of terrorism is an indication of how quickly the final events predicted in Revelation can loom up before us. It is time for those who hold a Biblical faith to be separate from the spirit and unholy practices of the age and to be obedient to all of God's requirements.

The youth culture that is based upon rock music, body piercing and adornment, cinema, sports and other forms of hedonism, has nothing to offer the youth of the world in a time of profound crisis. So any church that thinks that it can meet the real needs of youth today by offering reviews of rock music, cinema and novels and profiles of sports personalities in its youth magazines is badly out of contact with reality. Young people need today what they have always needed—conversion to Jesus Christ, obedience to all of His requirements and a life of service for others. That is the life that will prepare them to be citizens of heaven when Jesus comes again.

The hours of human probation are slipping away. There is little time for youth to prepare for Jesus' second coming. Yet, the preparation that youth require to meet Jesus in peace is the same preparation needed by adults (Revelation 22:11-15). Jesus loves youth and wants them to recognize His claims upon their affections and their lives. He is willing to provide all the resources of heaven to assist youth to be ready. But youth must respond and put their energies into personal preparation and warning and encouraging other youth. Those who minister to youth today have a most solemn responsibility resting upon them.

Bibliography

Anderson, William, 1996. *The Face of Glory: Creativity, Consciousness and Civilization*. London: Bloomsbury.

Bacchiocchi, Samuele, ed. 2000. *The Christian and Rock Music: A Study on Biblical Principles of Music*. Berrien Springs, Biblical Perspectives.

Berry, Thomas, 1988. *The Dream of the Earth*. San Francisco: Sierra Club Books.

Bloom, Allan, 1988. *The Closing of the American Mind: How higher education has failed democracy and impoverished the souls of today's students*. London: Penguin Books.

Brasch, Rudy, 1989. *How Did Sports Begin?* Sydney: Collins Australia.

Brockett, Oscar, 1987. *History of the Theater* (Fifth Ed.). Boston: Allyn and Bacon.

Campbell, Joseph and William Moyers, 1988. *The Power of Myth*. Doubleday: New York.

Carroll, John, 1993. *Humanism: The Wreck of Western Culture*. London: Fontana Press.

Eisen, George, 1978, Games and Sporting Diversions of the North American Indians as Reflected in American Writings of the sixteenth and seventeenth centuries. *Canadian Journal of History of Sport* 9:58-85.

Fernández-Armesto, Felipe and Derek Wilson, 1996. *Reformation: Christianity and the World 1500-2000*. London: Bantam Press.

Finley, M. I., 1977. *The Ancient Greeks*. Harmondsworth: Penguin Books.

Frayling, Christopher, 1995. *Strange Landscape: A Journey Through The Middle Ages*. London: BBC Books.

Gasman, Daniel, 1971. *The Scientific Origins of National Socialism: Social Darwinism in Ernst Haeckel and the German Monist League*. London: McDonald.

Grenz, Stanley. 1996. *A Primer on Postmodernism*. Grand Rapids: Eerdmans.

Harker, Barry. 1996. *Strange Fire: Christianity and the Rise of Modern Olympism.* Rapidan: Hartland Publications.

Hartnoll, Phyllis, 1995. *The Theatre: A Concise History.* London: Thames and Hudson.

Huizinga, Johann, 1955. *Homo Ludens: a study of the play element in culture.* Boston: The Beacon Press.

Hunt, Norman. 1996. *Gods and Myths of the Aztecs: The History and Development of Mexican Culture.* Sydney: Universal International.

Husain, Shahrukh. 1996. *The Goddess.* London: Duncan Baird Publishers.

Jencks, Charles, 1996. *What is Post-Modernism?* (Fourth Ed.) London: Academy Editions.

Jenkyns, Richard. 1980. *The Victorians and Ancient Greece.* Oxford: Basil Blackwell.

Keys, David, 1999. *Catastrophe: An Investigation into the Origins of the Modern World.* London: Century,

Kraus, Richard. 1971. *Recreation and Leisure in Modern Society.* Englewood Cliffs: Prentice-Hall.

Levi, Peter and Elliott Porter, 1988. *The Greek World.* New York: Archcape Press.

Mandell, Richard, 1976. *The First Modern Olympics.* Berkeley: University of California Press.

Maybury-Lewis, David. 1992. *Millennium: Tribal Wisdom and the Modern World.* New York: Viking.

Measham, Terence, Elizabeth Spathari and Paul Donnelly, 2000. *1000 Years of the Olympic Games: Treasures of Ancient Greece.* Sydney: Powerhouse Publishing.

McIntosh, Peter. 1963. *Sport in Society.* London: C. A. Watts.

Miracle, Andrew and Roger Rees, 1994. *Lessons of the Locker Room: The Myth of School Sports.* New York: Prometheus Books.

Murray, Alexander, 1988. *Who's Who in Mythology: Classic Guide to the Ancient World.* London: Bracken Books.

Olivová, Věra, 1984. *Sports and Games in the Ancient World.* London:

Orbis.

Peat, David. 1994. *Blackfoot Physics: A Journey into the Native American Universe*. London: Fourth Estate.

Pollitt, Herbert, 1996. *The Inter-Faith Movement: The New Age enters the Church*. Edinburgh: Banner of Truth Trust.

Poliakoff, Michael, 1987. *Combat Sports in the Ancient World: Competition, Violence, and Culture*. New Haven: Yale University Press.

Rosen, Roger, and Patra McSharry, eds. 1992. *Good Sports: Fair Play and Foul*. New York: The Rosen Publishing Group.

Sasajima, Kohsuke, 1988, History of Physical Education and Sport in Ancient Japan. *Canadian Journal of History of Sport* 19:57-61.

Steed, Ernest, 1978. *Two Be One: The Revealed Secrets of Long Hidden Mysticism and Religion*. Plainfield: Logos International.

Swaddling, Judith. 1992. *The Ancient Olympic Games*. London: British Museum Press.

Veith, Jr. Gene, 1994. *Postmodern Times: A Christian Guide to Contemporary Thought and Culture*. Wheaton: Crossway Books.

Walter, Nita, 1973. "Orcheisthai" – Ancient Greek Dance: The Origin of the Theater. *Canadian Journal of History of Sport and Physical Education* 4:63-75.

Zeigler, Earle, ed. 1973. *A History of Sports and Physical Education to 1900*. Champaign: Stipes.

General Index

actors; 25, 29, 35, 44, 78, 125
acupuncture; 84
Adam and Eve; 14-16
addictions; 52, 54, 92-95
Ahab; 129
Alexandria; viii
Alps, Cottian; ix
Altis, Sacred, Olympia; 3
ambassadors; 41
anarchism; 55
animism and spiritism; 38, 60
antediluvian period; 15, 116
antinomianism; 55, 111
Antioch; 122
apostasy; 22, 105, 106, 129
Aristotle; 25, 26
Arnaud, Antonin; 26
Arnold, Matthew; viii
arts
  deceptive; 46
  decorative; 83
  Greco-Roman; v
  magical; 45
  music, most powerful of; 68
  performance; 82
  popular culture and; 99
  Protestant era; ix
  visual, ancient Greece; 20
Assam, India; 13
astrology; 19

athleticism, Greek; vi, viii, 5, 6, 20, 21, 22, 27
Augustine; viii
Aztecs; 9
Baal, prophets of; 37, 81
Babel, Tower of; 16
Babylon; 33
Bach, Johann Sebastian; ix
ball court; 8, 9
ball game; 7-10, 19
Bathsheba; 75
beast; 33, 69, 70, 106
Bible; passim
bioregionalism; 38
blasphemy; 33, 69, 73
Bloom, Allan; 51-58, 61
body piercing and decoration; 65, 73, 81-84
Brazil; 10, 12, 13
British Museum; 18
British public schools; 1
bull leaping; 4, 5
bull rhyton; 4, 5
Bunyan, John; ix
Carmel, Mount; 37
Carthage, Council of; 30
cartoons; 119
cat's cradle; 10
Chardin, Pierre Teilhard de; 67, 68

cheating; 23
Chichen Itzá; 8
chronological snobbery; 101
cinema and movies; x, 32, 74, 76-78, 85, 91, 93, 124, 131
City Dionysia; 25
Clement; viii
clowning; x, 41-43, 82, 85
clowns; 11, 41-43, 125
Coliseum; 44
Colossians; v
comedians; 42, 125
comedy; vii, ix, x, 25-28, 31, 32, 38-41, 43, 45, 46, 49, 89
Communism; 58, 71
competition; vii, viii, 1, 2, 5, 12, 19, 20, 21, 26, 27, 32. 33, 40, 59, 127
compromise; viii, ix, x, xi, 2, 30, 69, 73, 112, 114, 121, 122, 123
Contemporary Christian Music; 52, 55
Corinth; vi, vii
cosmetics; 81-84
Coubertin, Baron Pierre de; 2
Counter-Reformation; 31
Creation; 16, 20, 48
Crete; 4, 5
criticism, Biblical; 58, 65
criticism, higher; ix
cultural relevance; i, x, xi-xiii, 49, 115
culture; Judeo-Christian; viii, 28, 36
Dainzú, Mexico; 9
dance; 24, 36-39, 42, 54, 58, 60, 63
  animist and spiritist; 38
  cosmic; 37
  Dionysian; 24
  dithyrambic chorus and; 25
  Jewish; 36, 38
  liturgical, rejection of; 38
  masks and; 43
  mimetic; 26, 44
  Muses and; 37
  possession and; 57, 60
  rave; 60
  satyrs and; 24
  sympathetic magic and; 37
  worship and; 36, 37
Daniel, the prophet; 33
Darwin, Charles; 57ff
Darwinism; ix, 58, 65
David; 36, 37, 75, 107, 119, 124
Death Gods; 7, 8
delusion; xii, xiii, 76, 77, 97, 99, 117
Demeter Chamyne; 5
democracy; 70, 71
Dionysus or Bacchus; vii, 24-26, 34
discernment; 71, 76, 77, 97, 115, 118
discipleship; 118, 120, 127
discus throwing; 6

Index

disobedience; 74, 107
dithyramb; 24, 25, 27
divination; 13, 19
doctrine; 66, 77, 102, 103, 110
dominion theology; 99, 100
dragon; 69
drama; x, 24-27, 30, 34-36, 43, 46, 49, 85
  ancient Greek; vii, 26, 28
  comedy and; 25, 27
  contemporary; 28, 35
  dance and; 36, 38
  emergence of; 34
  emotions and; 35
  liturgical; 30, 35
  Northern Europe, religious; ix, 31
  pastoral; 31
  sacred precincts and; 34
dress; 83ff
drugs; 54, 58, 59, 73, 93, 95
dualism; 13, 14, 16, 39
Ecstasy, drug; 60
ecstasy; 27, 37, 38, 55
ecumenism; x, 2, 31, 32, 66
education, liberal; 53, 54, 59
Elijah message; 126
Elijah; 129
Elisha; 128
emotions; 26, 35, 38, 51, 65, 87, 89
Enlightenment, The; 51, 55
enlightenment; 17, 91

Ephesians; 45
Eskimos; 10
evangelism; i, ix-xii, 28, 34-36, 39, 50, 53, 61, 62, 64, 66, 68, 88, 112, 113, 116-118, 122, 123, 128
evolution, theistic; 67
fascism; 58
feathered serpents; 18
fertility rites; vii, 3, 5, 18, 19, 26, 38
festivals
  Aiora; 38
  Anthesteria; 38
fire-eaters; 42
focussed evolution; 67
folly; 41, 42
Fortuna, Lady; 94
funeral games; 4
gambling; 11, 73, 93, 94
games and Games
  burial ceremonies and; 11
  cultic association of; 13
  death and; 4
  fertility and; 6, 19
  funeral; 4, 11
  gambling and; 11
  Isthmian; vi
  of chance; 11, 94
  Olympic; vi, 1-5, 21, 22
  origin of; 14, 19
  Pan-Hellenic; 19, 21
  ritual and; 19

seasonal; 10
symbolism of; 19
team; 13, 14
vegetation prizes and; 19
Ge; Earth goddess; 3
global youth culture; 59
globalization; 69
God; passim
golden calf; vi, 37, 105, 106
good and evil, union of; 17
gospel; i, xi, xii, 29, 34, 35, 42, 44, 45, 49, 50, 74, 78, 86, 89, 90, 91, 97, 103, 108, 118, 122, 123, 124, 126, 127, 128
Greater Dionysia; vii
Greece, ancient; ii, vi, 6, 9, 13, 20-22, 28, 31, 33, 36, 39, 42-44, 46, 65, 71
Greeks, Archaic; 39
group think; 81, 115, 116
groups, encounter and discussion; 91
gymnasia; vii
gymnos; 20
Haeckel, Ernst; 57, 58
Hebraism; viii
hedonism; ix, 131
Hellenism; viii
Hera; Temple of; 3
Holocaust; 58
Homer; 4
homoeroticism; 20
homosexuality; vii
human potential movement; 79, 80
Hunapa and Xbalanque; 7
ideas, Platonic; viii
idolatry; v, vi, vii, 36, 114
Iliad; 4
illusionists; 42, 45
imagination; 15, 40, 46, 54, 77, 78, 93, 94, 98, 110
  addiction and; 94
  comic; 40
  earthly; 77
  humane; 54
  mythic; 48, 49, 52
  Romantic; 52, 65
immortality, natural; 16, 17
Indians; 11
  Mandan; 80
  North American; 10, 11, 12, 80
  Hopi; 11
  Pueblo; 11, 42
  Timbira; 12
innovation; i, 16, 92, 100-102, 112, 122, 123
Inter-Faith Movement; 71
irrationalism; 52, 57, 58
Jagger, Mick; 57
Japan; 12, 80
Jencks, Charles; 66, 67
Jerusalem; 36
Jesus Christ; iv, v, 34, 35, 40, 99, 105, 108, 130, 131, passim

jewelry; 81-85, 91
John Mark; 120, 121
jokes; 7, 40, 119
Joseph; 119
Joshua; 105
Judeo-Christianity; viii, 28
jugglers; 42
Justinian II; 30
Kohlberg, Lawrence; 90
komos; 26
kordax; 38
leadership profiling; 91
Lewis, C. S; 101
log race; 12
Lords of the Dead; 7, 8
Luke; 74
Macuilxochitl; 9
magic
  fertility; 5
  mimetic or sympathetic; 9, 10, 13, 19, 37
magicians; 43, 125
  Christian; 45
Manual Labor movement; 2
marionettes; 43-45
Martyr, Justin; viii
mascara; 81
masks; 26, 27, 43, 44
Massingham, Harold John; 13, 14
materialism; ix
Maya; 7-9
Medo-Persia; 33

Megara; 26
Mesoamerica; 7-10
metaphor; vi, vii, 22
Milton, John; ix
mime, mimes; x, 26, 29, 30, 38, 41, 42, 44
mimesis; 3, 19, 26, 27
Moche temple; 45
modernism; 32, 51, 52, 65, 66
moieties; 10, 11, 12, 19
moral development, stage theories of; 90
Moses; 105, 110, 113
Mount Olympus; 3
Muscular Christianity; 1, 20, 22
music; passim
  beat; 104
  Dionysian; x, 65, 123
  rock; i, ii, x, 52-65, 68, 71, 73, 74, 91, 93, 99, 100, 101, 104, 105, 111, 112, 113, 115, 117, 123-127, 131
mythology; 3, 16, 17, 19, 24, 25, 27, 43, 65
myths; vii, 17, 19, 20, 22. 26, 28, 34, 35, 43, 65
nakedness; 14, 20
National Archaeological Museum of Athens; 6
Neuro-Linguistic Programming; 90
New Age movement; 67, 68,

79, 80, 91, 108
New Counter-Reformation; 66, 67
New Protestant Reformation; 66
New Testament; v, 22, 41, 45, 107
Nietzsche, Friedrich; 54, 55, 57
Nigeria, Nigerians; 10, 43
nihilism; 52, 57, 58, 103
obedience; iv, v, viii, ix, xii, 15, 35, 97, 107, 108, 115, 125, 131
occult, occultism; 18, 45
Old comedy; 26
Old Testament; iv, 35, 38, 45
Olympia; 3, 5, 6, 9
One Death; 7
opposites, conjunction of; 17, 25
Origen; viii
paganism; viii, ix, 3, 30, 33, 36, 43, 50, 70, 82, 113, 114
palaestra; 20
Palestine; 29, 126
pantheism; 67, 68
paralogy; 62, 98
Patroklos, funeral games of; 4
Paul and Barnabas; 121
Paul; v-vii, 41, 74, 106, 107, 123
pederasty; vii
Pelops; 4
personality typing; 91
Peru; 45

Peter; 122, 129
Philistines; 107
philosophers, Greek; 48
philosophy; v, viii, 20, 32, 47, 79, 81, 109, 124
Plato, platonism; viii, 27, 47, 54, 55
plays; 28, 30
 folk; 30, 31
 miracle; ix, 31, 43
 morality; 27, 30, 31, 43
 satyr; 25
pluralism; 57, 110
poetry, tragic; 47
Pok-ta-pok; 9
postmodernism; 51, 52, 57, 58, 62, 66, 67
prophet, false; 33, 69
prostitution; 18, 82
Protestantism; ix, 2, 31, 32, 33, 34, 68
psychology, humanistic; 91
Punch and Judy; 45
Puppets, puppeteers; 42, 44, 45
Quetzacoatl, Temple of; 18
rebellion; 15, 16, 19, 20, 57, 63, 82, 101, 105, 129
Reformation, Protestant; ix, x, 31
regeneration, theme of; 4, 6
Rehoboam; 120
relevance; 28, 29, 63, 102, 103, 113

religion, Eastern; 65
Republic, Plato's; 54
restoration; xii, 33, 118, 125
revelation; 16, 17, 20, 48, 49, 51, 65, 68, 98, 111
Roman Catholic Church; 30, 31, 67
Romans; 29
Rome; v, viii, 18, 42, 44, 94
Rousseau, Jean Jacques; 55
sacrifices; 3, 5, 7, 11, 13, 18, 19
salvation; iv, xii, 15, 31, 66, 77, 91, 99, 108, 109, 111, 113, 117, 118
Samuel; 119
Satan; 69, 77, 78, 83, 86, 87, 99, 117
satire; 39, 40
satyr; 2vii, 24, 25, 34, 57, 65
Schopenhauer, Arthur; 68
science, evolutionary; 67
scribes and Pharisees; 96
Second Coming; xiii, 131
secularization; 6, 19, 20
Sekaquaptewa, Emory; 43
self-esteem; 78, 79, 89, 93
Semele; 34
Seven Death; 7
shamans, shamanism; 38, 43, 91
Silenus; 25
Sinai, Mount; 37, 105
Socialism, National; 57

Socrates; 27, 46-49, 54
Solomon; 120
sorceries and enchantments; 45
spiritism and spiritualism; 44, 70, 91
spirituality; 41, 75, 85
  animist and spiritist; 60
  cosmic; 66
  global or world; 67-69
  New Age; 67, 80
  North American Indian; 80
  Protestant; 66
sports, extreme; 59, 73, 74, 78-81
sportsmanship; 1, 22
Stephen; iv
stewardship; 126, 128
Sumo; 12
sun worship; 18, 19
synagogue, temple; 36, 37, 78
Synod, Trullan; 30
Ten Commandments; 105
Tersichore; 37
theater; vii, viii, x, 26, 27, 28, 29, 30, 44, 47, 49, 73, 88, 115, 117, 122, 123, 125-127
  ancient Greek; 24, 27, 28, 31, 34, 46
  agonism in; 27
  at Caesarea; 29
  comic; 43
  contemporary; 24
  medieval; 31

mimes and; 44
modern; 28, 31
origin of; 24, 25, 28, 46
pagan; 30
Roman; 29, 30, 44, 46
sacred precincts; 34
tragic; 47
Western; 24, 28
Thucydides; 21
Timothy; 74, 109
Tlachtli; 9
tradition; iv, v, ix, 42, 51, 53, 63, 69, 81, 97
tragicomedy; 39, 46
tunica molesta; 44
Twin heroes; 7, 8
Tyche; 94, 95
tyranny; viii, 52, 57, 58, 66, 69, 71
University of Chicago; 51
University of New England, Australia; 55, 56
Urania; 38
Uzzah; 107
Van Rijn, Rembrandt; ix
Vatican Museum; 94
vegetation prizes; 5, 19
Waldenses; ix
Wichita tribe; 10
winning, athletic; 5, 11, 21, 22, 94
wizardry; 47
worldview
 ancient Greek; 11, 22, 24, 28, 38, 39, 46
 Christian; 21, 22, 35
 evolutionary; 103
 Roman; 46
 scientific; 60
worship; passim
Xavante, Brazil; 10, 12
Xibalba; 8ff
Young Men's Christian Association; 2
youth leaders; 86, 98, 102, 115, 117, 119, 121, 122, 128, 130
Yucatán Peninsula; 8
Zeus; vi, 3, 5, 34
Zuñis, Mexico; 10

Scriptural Index

Old Testament

Genesis 2:16, 17	16	Psalms 95:6	35
Genesis 3:4	16	Psalms 101:3	75
Genesis 3:5	17	Psalms 119:105	98
Genesis 3:6	17	Psalms 119:160	16
Exodus 32:7	105	Psalms 149:3	37
Exodus 32:19, 25	105	Psalms 150:2	37
Exodus 34:5-7	111	Proverbs 3:6	129
Leviticus 10:10	34	Proverbs 16:25	42
Leviticus 19:28	81	Proverbs 23:7	97
Deuteronomy 13:1-5	70	Ecclesiastes 2:13	41
Deuteronomy 14:1	81	Ecclesiastes 5:1, 2	87
Deuteronomy 18:10-12	45	Ecclesiastes 11:9, 10	117
Deuteronomy 22:5	85	Ecclesiastes 12:1	117
Deuteronomy 30:19, 20	94	Isaiah 1:18	48, 66, 87, 97
Judges 5:23	129	Isaiah 1:19, 20	97
1 Samuel 15:22	35	Isaiah 5:20	41, 76
1 Samuel 16:7	83	Isaiah 8:19, 20	70
1 Kings 12:3, 4	120	Isaiah 42:16	129
1 Kings 18:17, 18	129	Isaiah 43:25	xii
1 Kings 18:28	81	Isaiah 55:8, 9	48
2 Kings 2:23, 24	128	Isaiah 59:2	xii
2 Kings 9:30	81	Jeremiah 4:30	81
Job 31:1, 7	75	Jeremiah 6:16	92, 102
Psalms 34:10	94	Jeremiah 7:18	3
Psalms 42:7	118	Jeremiah 16:6	81
Psalms 51:10-12	124	Jeremiah 17:9	79, 106
Psalms 71:17	119	Ezekiel 3:8, 9	129
Psalms 84:11	94	Ezekiel 23:40	81
		Ezekiel 33:7-9	129
		Ezekiel 33:30-33	38

Daniel Chapter 2	33	John 17:15-17	iv, xi, 97
Daniel 2:20-22	94	Acts 2:17	119
Daniel Chapter 7	33	Acts 3:19	xii
Hosea 2:13	83	Acts 3:20, 21	xii
Hosea 4:6	102	Acts 5:29	129
Malachi 4:5, 6	126	Acts Chapter 17	49
		Acts 17:23	48
New Testament		Acts 19:1-20	45
		Acts 20:27	121
Matthew 4:5, 6	78	Romans 2:7	15
Matthew 4:8-11	99	Romans 2:13	108
Matthew 5:27, 28	75	Romans 8:1-14	xii
Matthew 5:48	xii, 15	Romans 8:29	xii, 49
Matthew 7:21-29	xii, 15, 108	Romans 14:17	119
Matthew 12:25	42	1 Corinthians 1:21	49
Matthew 15:9	97	1 Corinthians 2:9	77
Matthew 24:14	xi	1 Corinthians 2:10	118
Matthew 25:14-30	79	1 Corinthians 6:9-11	vii
Matthew 26:30	126	1 Corinthians 6:9, 10, 12	29
Matthew 28:19, 20	xi	1 Corinthians 6:20	78
Mark 5:1-20	82	1 Corinthians 9:22	28, 122
Luke 5:21	69	1 Corinthians 9:24-27	vi
Luke 5:22	96	1 Corinthians 10:1-11	vi, vii, 106
Luke 6:46	xii		
Luke 17:26-30	116	1 Corinthians 10:14	vi
Luke 18:8	74	1 Corinthians 14:20	87
Luke 19:13	126	1 Corinthians 14:33	40, 66
John 1:14	48	1 Corinthians 15:51-56	xiii
John 4:23	107	2 Corinthians 3:17	82
John 7:17	77, 97	2 Corinthians 3:18	49, 75
John 10:10	106	2 Corinthians 5:20	126
John 10:33	69	2 Corinthians 13:5	79
John 14:6	91, 109	2 Corinthians 13:8	130

Index

Galatians 2:11-14	122	1 John 3:4	xii
Ephesians 4:15	129	1 John 5:1-5	v
Ephesians 4:18	76	Jude 13	98
Ephesians 5:11	45	Revelation Chapter 13	33, 66, 69
Philippians 2:5	125		
Philippians 4:8	75	Revelation 13:4	69
Colossians 2:8	v	Revelation 13:6	69
Colossians 3:1-3	125	Revelation 13:11-17	116
1 Thessalonians 5:23	79	Revelation 13:15-17	69
2 Thessalonians 2:4	69	Revelation 13:18	69
2 Thessalonians 2:15	114	Revelation 14:6, 7	103
1 Timothy 2:9	83	Revelation 14:8-11	103, 106
1 Timothy 4:12	119	Revelation 14:12	108
2 Timothy 1:9	41	Revelation 16:13	69
2 Timothy 2:22	74	Revelation 17:5	70
2 Timothy 3:1-5	74	Revelation 17:13	70
2 Timothy 3:13	74	Revelation 22:11-15	xii, 131
2 Timothy 3:14, 15	74		
2 Timothy 4:2	110		
2 Timothy 4:4	35		
2 Timothy 4:11	121		
Hebrews 4:12	49		
1 Peter 1:23	49, 87		
1 Peter 2:9, 10	iv		
1 Peter 2:11	106		
1 Peter 2:20, 21	104		
1 Peter 3:1-5	83		
1 Peter 3:15	96		
1 Peter 5:5	86		
1 Peter 5:8	87		
2 Peter 1:20	96		
1 John 2:15-17	v, xi		
1 John 2:16	76		

HARTLAND PUBLICATIONS PUBLISHED BOOK LIST

Books by Colin and Russell Standish

The Antichrist Is Here $10.95 PB 185 pgs.
A newly updated, second edition! Colin and Russell Standish have extensively researched the historical identification of the Antichrist of past generations and are convinced the Antichrist is present on earth now. A "must-read" for those who are interested in Biblical prophecy and its outworking in contemporary history.

The Big Bang Exploded $11.95 PB 218 pgs.
A refutation of the Big Bang theory and Darwin's proposal of natural selection, and boldly presents evidence that supports, far more closely, the fiat creation concept than the evolutionary model.

Education for Excellence $11.95 PB 176 pgs.
This book goes directly to the word of God for educational principles for the sons and daughters of the King of the Universe.

The Entertainment Syndrome $8.95 PB 126 pgs.
This book explores how entertainment impacts the physical, emotional, social, intellectual and spiritual life of the human race, and the devasting effect of its use in our churches.

The Evangelical Dilemma $10.95 PB 222 pgs.
There has never been a more urgent time for an honest review of the past, present and future of Evangelical Protestantism. The authors present an examination of the major doctrinal errors of Evangelical Protestants.

Georgia Sits On Grandpa's Knee (R. Standish) $7.95 PB 86 pgs.
Stories for children based on the experience of Russell and his children

in the mission field.

God's Solution for Depression, Guilt and Mental Illness $12.95 PB 229 pgs.
This powerful book argues with great persuasiveness that God is interested in every aspect of His created beings and that the perfect answers to all of man's needs are to be found in the Word of God.

Grandpa, You're Back! (R. Standish) $9.95 PB 128 pgs.
Pastor Russell Standish again delights and fascinates his granddaughter, Georgia, with stories of his many travels to countries ranging from South America to such far-flung places as Singapore, Africa, and beyond. These stories should pleasantly awake the imagination of young readers.

Gwanpa and Nanny's Home (R. Standish and Ella Rankin) $14.95 PB 128 pgs.
"I am Ella Marie Rankin. I want to tell you about Gwanpa's and Nanny's home. But I have a problem! You see, I'm only three and I haven't yet learned to write. So, my Gwanpa is writing my story for me." So begins a book that Russell Standish wrote for his Granddaughter.

Holy Relics or Revelation $14.95 PB 300 pgs.
Biblical archaeologists have gathered data with painstaking effort, their work proving the accuracy of the Bible. Yet, mostly within a single decade, Ron Wyatt had sought out and claimed the most amazing Biblical sites and relics. In this book, the Standish Brothers examine the Wyatt claims in-depth. Their findings serve as a benchmark upon which Ron Wyatt's "discoveries" can be more carefully evaluated.

Liberty in the Balance $14.95 PB 263 pgs.
The bloodstained pathway to religious and civil liberty faces its greatest test in 200 years. The United States "Bill of Rights" lifted the concept of liberty far beyond the realm of toleration to an inalienable right for all citizens. Yet, for a century and a half, some students of the prophecies of John the Revelator have foretold a time just prior to the return of Christ

when these most cherished freedoms will be wrenched from the citizens of the United States, and. the U.S. would enforce its coercive edicts upon the rest of the world. This book traces the courageous battle for freedom, a battle stained with the lives of many martyrs.

The Lord's Day $15.95 PB 310 pgs.
The issue of the apostolic origin of Sunday worship had often been a contentious one between Roman Catholics and Protestants. This book presents an in-depth examination of the Sabbath in Scripture.

Modern Bible Translations Unmasked $10.95 PB 228 pgs.
This is book will challenge the reader to consider two very serious problems with modern Bible translations: first, the use of corrupted Greek manuscripts; and second, translational bias. This is a must read for anyone interested the veracity and accuracy of the Word of God.

The Mystery of Death $10.95 PB 128 pgs.
There are those today who believe that the soul is immortal and externally preexisted the body. Pagan or Christian, the opinions vary widely. In this book, the history of these concepts is reviewed and the words of Scripture are investigated for a definitive and unchallengeable answer.

Perils of Ecumenism $15.95 PB 416 pgs.
The march of ecumenism seems unstoppable. From its humble roots after the first World War, with the formation of the Faith and Order Council at Edinburgh University, Scotland, and the Works and Labor Council at Oxford University, England, to the formation of the World Council of Churches in 1948 in Amsterdam, it has gained breathtaking momentum. The authors see the ecumenical movement as very clearly identified in Holy Scriptures as the movement devised by the arch-deceiver to beguile the inhabitants of the world.

The Pope's Letter and Sunday Law $7.95 PB 116 pgs.
A detailed examination of John Paul II's apostolic letter, "Dies Domini."

The Rapture and the Antichrist (Pre-publication)
This book sets forth the plainest truths of Scripture directing Protestantism back to its Biblical roots. It will challenge the thinking of all Christians, erase the fictions of the Left Behind Series, and plant the readers' spiritual feet firmly on the platform of Scripture.

The Rapture, the End Times and the Millennium (Pre-publication)
This book will open the minds of the readers to a clear understanding of areas of the end-time which have led to much perplexity among laypeople and theologians alike. It is also guaranteed to dispel many of the perplexities presently confronting those who are searching for a clear Biblical exposition of the last cataclysmic days in which we now live.

The Sacrificial Priest $15.95 PB 272 pgs.
To all Christians the centrality of the sacrifice of Christ on Calvary has been the focus of their hopes of salvation. However, relatively few Christians have understood the equally important ministry of Christ in the heavenly sanctuary. The authors provide a fascinating Biblical explanation and irrefutable evidence of this little-studied high priestly ministry of Christ in the heavenly sanctuary.

The Second Coming $7.95 PB 80 pgs.
The Apostle Paul refers to the second coming of Jesus as the blessed hope (Titus 2:12). Yet, soon after the death of the apostles, doubts and debates robbed the people of this assurance and brought in the pagan notion of immediate life after death. In this new updated work, Colin and Russell Standish present a "wake-up call" for every complacent Christian.

Two Beasts, Three Deadly Wounds and Fourteen Popes $16.95 PB 234 pgs.
The Book of Revelation has been characterized as a mystery. Yet, the book describes itself as the "Revelation of Jesus Christ" (Revelation 1:1). In this book, Russell and Colin Standish, using Scripture as its own interpreter, unravel aspects of the "mystery" and unveil a portion of the revelation.

The Vision and God's Providence (C. Standish) $12.95 PB 176 pgs.
The story of the development of Hartland Institute must be attributed to God alone. Yet, many men and women have had the privilege of being His humble instruments in contributing to Hartland's establishment. This book recalls divine leadings, human weakness, misunderstandings, and strong differences of opinion, and we cannot but wonder what God might have accomplished, had we listened perfectly to His voice.

Youth Do You Dare! (C. Standish) $6.95 PB 74 pgs.
If you are a young person looking for workable answers to the many issues that confront you today, this book is for you. It presents a call to young people to follow truth and righteousness, and to live morally upright lives.

Other Books from Hartland Publications

Behold the Lamb - David Kang $8.95 PB 107 pgs.
God's plan of redemption for this world and the preservation of the universe is revealed in the sanctuary which God constructed through Moses. This book explains the sanctuary service in the light of the Christian's personal experience.

Christ and Antichrist - Samuel J. Cassels $24.95 HB 348 pgs.
First published in 1846 by a well-known Presbyterian minister, who called this book "not sectarian, but a Christian and Protestant work." He hoped that the removal of obstacles might result in a more rapid spread of the Gospel. One of these obstacles he saw as Antichristianity," a term that he used to described the Papal system.

Distinctive Vegetarian Cuisine -Sue M. Weir $14.95 PB 329 pgs.
100% vegan cooking, with no animal products—no meat, milk, eggs, cheese, or even honey. No irritating spices or condiments are used. Most of the ingredients can be found at your local market. There are additional nutritional information and helpful hints. Make your dinner table appealing to the appetite!

Food for Thought - Susan Jen $10.95 PB 160 pgs.
Where does the energy which food creates come from? What kinds of foods are the most conductive to robust health and well being in all dimensions of our life? What is a balanced diet? Written by a healthcare professional, this book examines the food we prepare for our table.

Group Think - Horace E. Walsh $5.95 PB 96 pgs.
Find out how a state of groupthink (or group dynamics) has often contributed to disaster in secular and spiritual matters, like the role of Hebrew groupthink in the rejection and ultimate crucifixion of the Son of God. Or, the Ecumenical Movement that seeks to unite the minds of dedicated men so much that their passion is to build one great super church following Rome.

Heroes of the Reformation - Hagstotz and Hagstotz $14.95 PB 320 pgs.
This volume brings together a comprehensive picture of the leaders of the Reformation who arose all over Europe. The authors of this volume have made a sincere endeavor to bring the men of Protestantism alive in the hearts of this generation.

His Mighty Love - Ralph Larson $9.95 PB 159 pgs.
Twenty-one evangelistic sermons! Every doctrine of the Bible is simply an answer to the question, "How does the love of God relate to this particular question or problem?" Every doctrine is further evidence that God is love! This book is divided into three sections with seven individual sermons each. Subjects range from "If God Is Almighty, Why Does He Permit Sin?" to "The Unpardonable Sin."

History of the Gunpowder Plot - Philip Sidney $13.95 PB 303 pgs.
Originally published on the 300th anniversary of the November 5, 1605, plot aimed at the destruction of the English Realm, Philip Sydney's account of one of the most audacious conspiracies ever known to the ancient or modern world. The failed plot became part of English popular culture.

The History of Protestantism - J. A. Wylie $99.95 PB 4 Volumes
This book pulls back the divine curtain and reveals God's hand in the affairs of His church during the Protestant Reformation. Your heart will be stirred by the lives of Protestant heroes, and your mind captivated by God's simple means to counteract the intrigues of its enemies. As God's church faces the last days, this compelling book will appeal to all who love the truth, and will be a blessing to adults as well as children.

History of the Reformation of the 16th Century - J. d'Aubigné $19.95 PB 876 pgs.
In history and in prophecy, the Word of God portrays the long continued conflict between truth and error. Today we see an alarming lack of understanding in the Protestant Church concerning the cause and effect of the Reformation. This reprinted masterpiece pulls back the curtain of history and divine providence to reveal the true catalyst for the Reformation—God's Word and His Holy Spirit.

History of the Reformation in the Time of Calvin - d'Aubigné $129.95 4 Vols.
The renovation of the individual, of the Church, and of the human race, is the theme. This renovation is, at the same time, an enfranchisement; and we might assign, as a motto to the Reformation accomplished by Calvin, as well as to apostolical Christianity itself, these words of Jesus Christ: The truth shall make you free (John 8:32).

History of the Waldenses - J. A. Wylie $12.95 PB 191 pgs.
During the long centuries of papal supremacy, the Waldenses defied the crushing power of Rome and rejected its false doctrines and traditions. This stalwart people cherished and preserved the pure Word of God. It is fitting that this edition of their history should be reprinted to keep alive the spirit and knowledge of this ancient people.

Hus the Heretic - Poggius the Papist $9.95 PB 78 pgs.
One of the greatest of Reformers in history was John Hus. His pious life and witness during his trial and martyrdom convinced many of the

priests and church leaders of his innocence and the justice of his cause. Poggius was the papal legate who delivered the summons to Hus to appear at the council of Constance, then participated as a member. This book consists of letters from Poggius to his friend Nikolai, and describes the trial and burning of Hus. So potent was John Hus' humble testimony, that even some of his ardent foes became his defenders.

The Law and the Sabbath - Allen Walker $9.95 PB 149 pgs.
A fierce controversy is swirling around the role the Ten Commandments should play in the church of the 21st Century. With a foreword by the late Elder Joe Crews, here is a book that dares to examine the Bible's own answers—with unfailing scriptural logic and a profound appreciation for the doctrine of righteousness by faith.

The Method of Grace - John Flavel $14.95 PB 458 pgs.
In this faithful reprint, John Flavel thoroughly outlines the work of God's Spirit in applying the redemptive work of Christ to the believer. Readers will find their faith challenged and enriched. In true Puritan tradition, a clearly defined theology is delivered with evangelistic fervor, by an author urgently concerned about the eternal destiny of the human soul.

My Escape from the Auto de Fe - Don Fernando de la Mina $9.95 PB 112 pgs.
In the difficult days of the Reformation in Spain, Nobleman Don Fernando de la Mina was arrested by the Inquisitors and sentenced to death for "heresy." He was about to be burned at the stake at the Auto de Fe´ (act of faith), when, through several incredible miracles of Providence, he made his escape. This captivating story will strengthen your faith in the protecting hand over God's faithful believers.

The Reformation in Spain - Thomas M'Crie $13.95 PB 272 pgs.
The boldness with which Luther attacked the abuses and the authority of the Church in Rome in the 16th Century attracted attention throughout Christendom. Luther's writings, along with the earlier ones

of Erasmus, gained a foothold with a Spanish people hungry for the truth. Thomas M'Crie makes a case for a Spain free of the religious errors and corruptions that ultimately dried up the resources and poisoned the fountains of a great empire.

Romanism and the Reformation - H. Grattan Guinness $12.95 PB 217 pgs.
The Reformation of the 16th Century, which gave birth to Protestantism, was based on Scripture. It gave back to the world the Bible. Such Reformation work needs to be done again today. The duty of diffusing information on the true character and history of "Romanism and the Reformation" is one that presses on God's faithful people in these days.

Strange Fire - Barry Harker $11.95 PB 206 pgs.
The Olympic games are almost universally accepted as a great international festival of peace, sportsmanship, and friendly competition. Yet, the games are riddled with conflict, cheating, and objectionable competitiveness. Discover the disturbing truth about the modern Olympics and the role of Christianity in the rise of this neo-pagan religion.

Truth Triumphant - Benjamin George Wilkinson $14.95 PB 419 pgs.
The prominence given to the "Church in the Wilderness" in the Scriptures establishes without argument its existence and emphasizes its importance. The same challenges exist today with the Remnant Church in its final controversy against the powers of evil to show the holy, unchanging message of the Bible.

Who Are These Three Angels? - Jeff Wehr $6.95 PB 126 pgs.
The messages of three holy angels unfold for us events that are soon to take place. Their warning is not to be taken lightly. They tell of political and religious movements that signal the soon return of Jesus.

Hartland Publication Books
True Education History Series from Hartland Publications

The Waldenses - The Church in the Wilderness $7.95 PB 72 pgs.
The faithful Waldenses in their mountain retreats were married in a spiritual sense to God who promised, "I will betroth thee unto me in faithfulness and thou shalt know the Lord" (Hosea 2:20). No invention of Satan could destroy their union with God. Follow the history of these people as they are compared to the dedicated eagle parents.

David Livingstone - The Pathfinder - Basil Matthews $8.95 PB 112 pgs.
Like most boys and girls, David Livingstone wondered what he would become when he grew up. He had heard of a brave man who was a missionary doctor in China. He also learned that this Dr. Gulztoff had a Hero, Jesus, who had come to people as a healer and missionary. David learned all about this great Physician, and felt that the finest thing in the whole world for him was to follow in the same way and be a medical missionary. That was David's quest. Between these pages, you shall see how he made his good wish come true.

Missionary Annals - Memoir of Robert Moffat - M. L. Wilder $7.95 PB 64 pgs.
Robert Moffat first heard from his wise and pious mother's lips that there were heathen in the world and of the efforts of Christians sharing the knowledge of a Savior who could raise them out of their base degradation. An intense desire took possession of him to serve God in some marked manner but how that would be, he did not know. Through a series of providential circumstances and in God's good time, the London Society accepted him as one of their missionaries, and in 1816, he embarked on his first trip to heathen Africa. This book will inspire young and old as you read the many trials, disappointments, triumphs, and the wondrous miracles that God accomplishes when one is fully surrendered to the Him.

HARTLAND PUBLICATIONS was established in 1984 as a conservative, self supporting Protestant publishing house. We publish Bible-based books and produce media for Christians of all ages, to help them in the development of their personal characters, always giving glory to God in preparation for the soon return of our Lord and Savior, Christ Jesus. We are especially dedicated to the reprinting of significant books on Protestant history that might otherwise go out of circulation. Hartland Publications supports and promotes other Christian publishers and media producers who are consistent with biblical principles of truth and righteousness. We are seeking to arouse the spirit of true Protestantism, that is based on the Bible and the Bible only, thus awakening the world to a sense of the value and privilege of the religious liberty that we currently enjoy.

HARTLAND PUBLICATIONS

Office hours: 9:00 a.m. to 5:00 p.m. Mon.— Thurs.,
9:00 a.m. to 12:00 noon Fri. (Eastern Standard Time)
Orders may be placed by telephone, fax, mail, e-mail or on the Internet

Payments in US funds by check, money order, most credit cards
Order line: 1-800-774-3566;   FAX 1-540-672-3568

Website: www.hartlandpublications.com
E-mail:sales@hartlandpublications.org